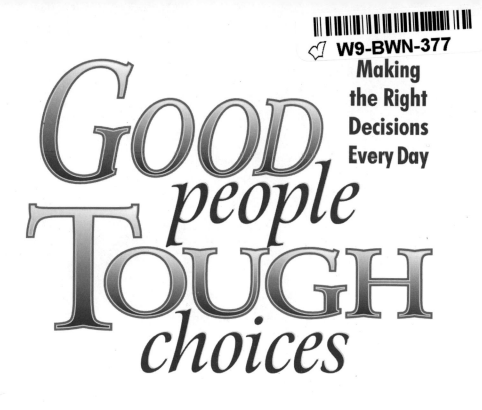

GOOD
people
TOUGH
choices

Making
the Right
Decisions
Every Day

Good people Tough choices

Making the Right Decisions Every Day

Timothy E. O'Connell, Ph.D.

ThomasMore®
– An RCL Company –
Allen, Texas

Cover Design by Melody Loggins, Zia Designs
Book Interior Design by Gregg Layton, Layton Graphics

Author photo on back cover by Pete Stenberg

Send all inquiries to: Distributed by BookWorld Services, Inc.
Thomas More®   1933 Whitfield Park Loop
An RCL Company   Sarasota FL 34243
200 East Bethany Drive   888/444-2524 or fax 800/777-2525
Allen, Texas 75002-3804   941/758-8094 or fax 941/753-9396

PARISHES AND SCHOOLS:
    Contact Thomas More Publishing 800-822-6701 or fax 800-688-8356
INTERNATIONAL:
    Fax Thomas More Publishing 972-264-3719

Visit our website at **www.rclweb.com**

Printed in the United States of America

Library of Congress Catalog Card Number 98–68123

ISBN 0-88347-427-0

1 2 3 4 5   03 02 01 00 99

To

J.F.D.
G.J.D.

Trailblazers and Guides

ACKNOWLEDGMENTS

The preparation of a book like this may appear a solitary work, arising from a single writer hunched over his word processor. I hope the briefest reading leads you to conclude that this is not the case. My 25 years of professional life have allowed me to drink from widely varied fountains of wisdom. I trust that my inability to name all these wonderful people, or in some cases even to recall their gifts, will not contradict the depth of my dependence and the genuineness of my gratitude.

I am especially grateful to the many women and men who, by telling me their stories or by allowing me to be present to their struggles, have provided the basis for the many stories in this book. In fairness to these wonderful people, however, I should hasten to add that I have consistently changed details in order to protect confidentiality. In some cases, indeed, I have modified the stories, both to further disguise their origin and for narrative focus.

The completion of this book has been graced with astute suggestions from several colleagues and friends. I want to offer thanks and praise to Mary Kaye Cisek, Barbara DeCoursey Roy, and William Huebsch. And most especially, I remain grateful for the astute suggestions of Larry Little, my most consistent and supportive critic.

I also want to acknowledge the generous assistance of Loyola University Chicago, which granted me a research leave during the fall 1998 semester, so that I could complete this book.

Finally, I grow in admiration for and appreciation of my compatriots at Thomas More Press. My publisher, John Sprague, has been consistently supportive and helpful, as have the other members of this publishing team. And my extraordinary editor, Debra Hampton, has been the source of both advice and encouragement without measure.

So much good has come from all these people. Mistakes found here, alas, are all mine.

TABLE OF CONTENTS

—❦—

—❦— —❦— —❦—

1

Everyday Struggles

She had a terrible decision to make; there was nothing she could do to avoid it. I was inspired to listen as she talked about her choices and asked for suggestions. I was humbled that I was being consulted. But mostly, I was pained as I watched her struggle with the dilemma she couldn't avoid.

I've known Mrs. Oatley and her husband since I was thirteen years old. Their son was a high school classmate of mine, one of my best friends, and we often spent time hanging around their house. I grew to love Mr. Oatley's lively bluster. His name was Charlie. We'd never dare call him that, but the name fit him to a T. And the calm, smiling welcome of Mrs. Oatley—if Grace hadn't been her name, we'd have had to give it to her—made us all feel like we were extended members of the family. We loved being at the Oatley's.

Now, here we are, forty years later, and I'm watching her face the toughest decision of her life. Charlie's had a series of small strokes. They've left him barely able to walk, able to care for himself only with help, communicative at times but mostly withdrawn. He's an old man now.

He's also 220 pounds. And for tiny, four-foot-ten Grace, that's just too much to handle. She's tried to. If she climbs up on the bed, she can get him organized. If she tugs in just the right way, she can get him on his feet. But if he falls—and he has—she can't possibly get him upright by herself.

There's no avoiding the choice. Grace has to make some sort of arrangements for Charlie. He just can't continue to live in the place that's been his home for a half-century.

As I listened to this woman, I had many thoughts. I shared some of them, perspectives I thought might help, options I thought she might want to consider, people she might want to consult. But one thought I kept to myself. This struggle that she was having, as painful as it was, as overwhelming as it was in the moment, was an everyday struggle.

I certainly don't mean that her struggle was easy. You've known people in circumstances like this, and you know it isn't easy. I don't mean it had a simple solution. To be honest, I'm not sure it had any solution at all. But it was, in the end, the kind of struggle we all have to face, the sort of tough choice that confronts all human persons from time to time in the course of the lives they live.

And curiously, if you're a good person, as Grace most certainly was, it doesn't make these tough choices any easier. In fact, in some strange way it makes them more difficult. Mean and nasty people can, I suppose, just ship their parents off to an institution, file them in some warehouse for humans, and never give it a moment's thought. Good people can't do that. So good people, most especially, face these tough choices squarely and attempt to deal honorably with the everyday struggles that they meet.

You can see where I'm going with this. I'm talking about the Oatleys and their troubles, sure. But I'm also talking about you, and I'm talking about me. Our everyday struggles may not be exactly like Grace's, but we have them nonetheless. Like her, we're good people—or at least we try to be. And with us, too, that doesn't make things any easier. So like her, but in our own very different ways, we're facing tough choices that just won't go away.

I don't know exactly what your tough choices are. But just as I was able to help Grace Oatley by listening, by understanding, and by making some carefully chosen suggestions, I can do the same for you. So I'm proposing that we walk awhile together, talking and thinking in these pages. I'm proposing that we give each other some time, perhaps in little pieces over the next days or weeks. I'm proposing that we see if we can find a better way.

This book is for us. It's for all of us good people who face tough choices. It's for all of us who want to find a better way to handle the everyday struggles of our lives.

⇒◆⇐

All of us humans have this experience of feeling caught by everyday struggles, and we don't like it. Sometimes it makes us feel guilty, sometimes it leaves us depressed. Regularly, it makes us feel frustrated. It's almost more than we can bear. In fact, for some folks it is more than they can bear. The burden of being caught by tough choices leads some people to bail out, to give up completely on the project of really loving their neighbor.

Some people bail out into a small world of self-indulgence. They settle for a feel-good approach to life. Oh, they're not mean people, not cruel or vicious. But they've bailed out just the same. They've decided that as long as they feel OK about their choices, nothing else counts.

"Tell me, Fred, what did you decide about your neighbor who plays that loud music late at night?" "I decided to call the police, and I feel really good about my decision." Or . . . "I decided to turn up the music on my own stereo, and I feel really good about my decision." Or . . . "I decided to throw a Molotov cocktail through my neighbor's window, and I feel really good about my decision."

The point is that people like this try to "wish" themselves out of their everyday struggles, substituting nice feelings for careful thinking. As long as Fred feels good about his decision, it makes no difference whether he phoned the police or bombed his neighbor's house. And if most examples are rarely this obvious, still the fact is that lots of people, nice people, handle their tough choices in just this way.

"I don't know who is really the better candidate for office. But I do know my friends will like me if I vote for this person, and being able to claim that vote will make me feel good. So it's done!" "I don't know if my company's practice of giving expensive Christmas gifts to vendors and customers is really honest. But my career certainly wouldn't be served by asking questions. So my strategy is clear!" "I don't know if supplying my kids with all the latest outfits really teaches them the right values. But all the other parents are getting them, and the kids will love me if I do, too. So, off to the store!"

These people have bailed out into a feel-good morality.

Other people deal with feeling caught in their everyday struggles another way. They flee into the empty world of rule-obeying. They trade the complexity of their own lives for the fake simplicity of someone else's rules. They decide that they'll follow those rules, whether or not this results in the good of the neighbor. These people bail out just as surely.

I'm as unhappy as the next person with the increasing craziness of drivers on the highway. But I'm no more happy with folks who stubbornly stick to the speed limit while cars jam up behind them. Nor am I happy about religious leaders who shout about the rules of their church when the issue isn't the good of persons or the worship of God, but merely the power of rules. And I'm most certainly not happy about those terrible cults seizing impressionable young people, and conning them into a life of blind obedience.

Like many people, I was stunned when I read the newspaper account of a man, a victim of a shooting, who died at the front door of a hospital emergency room. The staff refused to step outside and carry him in. Hospital policy, they said, prohibited their "leaving the premises" to provide medical care. The hospital administrator was embarrassed, and quickly revised the policy. I was appalled! It's hard to believe anyone would think that a rule could address all possible circumstances or that people could escape the pain of everyday struggles so easily.

But people do think this. They believe that, by committing themselves to the tidy standard of a rule, they can be spared the complexity of life and the pain of feeling caught. They either obeyed the rule or they didn't, these people think. It's that simple. But it's not.

These two simplicities, self-indulgence and rule-obeying, come at a price. The price is the good of my neighbor. Sometimes, by happy coincidence I may actually end up helping my neighbor by what I do in order to feel good or to obey some rule. But there's no guarantee that I will, and in any case helping my neighbor's no longer really my goal when I'm using these escapes. So the fact remains that when I remove my neighbor's well-being from the center of my attention and replace it with either of these other concerns, whether I will feel good or whether I will be able to justify myself by some rule, then I fail the challenge of being a good person.

So even though the experience of feeling caught by everyday struggles isn't pleasant, we shouldn't flee it in ways that betray our core commitment to our neighbor. We shouldn't abandon so easily the challenges of our everyday struggles. There simply has to be a better way for good people to face their tough choices.

In this book I'll present a better way. I know that you deal with everyday struggles. I know that you, as a good person who tries to do good things for yourself and for those who depend on you, face tough choices almost every day. For you, I will offer a better way.

In these pages, I won't present simple solutions that will blow away the clouds of our human struggles. That would be naive. And I suspect that if I tried to do that, you'd see through them and reject them as the false solutions they'd be. But I will present perspectives that will help us move through the complexities of our situations, traveling from uncertainty to a good decision.

After saying a few more things in this chapter about why we all have this experience of being caught, I'll turn our attention to various areas where everyday struggles most beleaguer people like you and me. I'll talk about spending money and raising children. I'll discuss the challenges of being sexual and the demands of being generous. I'll examine some of the tough choices that grow daily more common in the world of medicine and health care. I'll share experiences and insights about bringing love and honor into the world of work. I'll struggle with the everyday challenges of being an individual who is also a member of many communities.

In each of the following chapters I'll combine some helpful ideas with lots of examples. I'll tell you about inspiring people I've met, and I'll describe the courageous and clever ways they've handled their tough choices. Through these ideas—and even more through the examples of the people I'll tell you about—I'll offer some useful tools for the challenges of our own everyday struggles.

As we explore each of these areas you'll see yourself, I suspect. You'll hear stories of struggles that are the struggles you face. You'll consider examples of tough choices that are the tough choices you are considering. You'll see yourself as you are, and as you're hoping to be.

In all this, then, I'll respond to your experience of being caught. I'll help make this painful experience of yours—and of mine—less an encounter with despair and more a challenge to creativity and growth.

———◆———

Before we move to this discussion of various troubling areas of life, let me add one further set of thoughts. I've said that all of us have the experience of feeling caught, that we all face everyday struggles. Why is that? I think it's important to see the answer to this question.

The fact is that these everyday struggles are not simply the result of bad thinking or unusual circumstances. It's not that something's gone wrong, either in the outer world of events or in the inner world of our own efforts. Not at all. If anything, our experience of these struggles is evidence that we're completely normal, that our outer world is typical and our inner world is healthy. For the struggles we encounter are the result of being human, nothing more and nothing less. They come with the territory of being human, and so they're a burden we all share in the conduct of our ordinary lives. Consider the following two thoughts:

Why is it we so often feel trapped by unattractive options? One answer—and therefore one reason for this book—is a simple but also profound truth: as human beings all of us are finite. We're limited. Everything we do involves choices. And in every choice something is always left undone.

We spend money on this, and we have nothing to spend on that. We give time to one project, and we have no time for another. We commit ourselves to one person, and we are unavailable to others. In every choice of our lives we crash against the wall of our finitude, this limitedness that is part of being human.

Of course, dogs and cats are limited, too. The "choices" they make, picking Kennel Ration over Purina Dog Chow, for example, also involve giving up alternatives, just as ours do. But these choices don't seem to bother them the way they bother us. Dogs and cats don't seem to fret over the frustration of being caught by unattractive options.

The reason for that is also simple, and it is also profound, and this reason provides the second explanation of why this book is important. The reason is that, as human beings, all of us can still imagine the infinite. All the time that we experience our finitude in the tough choices that can't both be embraced, we also experience the attraction of just that sort of all-inclusiveness. I suppose that when Fido makes one choice, she doesn't continue to imagine the alternative, but we do! So the inadequacies of our choices are never lost to us. The fact that our options leave much good undone, and even cause some harm along the way, is a truth we can't help but notice.

For us humans, then, efforts to care for our neighbors suffer the pain of two intersecting truths: We're finite beings who nonetheless always imagine the infinite we can't attain. So for all of us, because we're human, because we're beings forced to make choices that exclude as well as include, and because in the moment of these choices we continue to see clearly in the theater of our imaginations the choice that's left undone, we feel caught.

It's not a pleasant experience, this sense of being caught. It may be some consolation to know that we all have the experience, but it doesn't remove the pain. What can remove the pain, or at least reduce it, is some careful thinking about the everyday struggles.

That's what the coming chapters will provide.

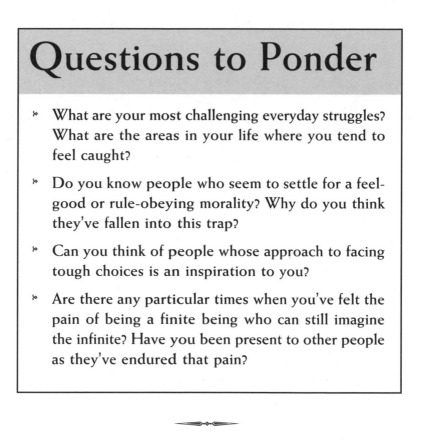

Questions to Ponder

* What are your most challenging everyday struggles? What are the areas in your life where you tend to feel caught?

* Do you know people who seem to settle for a feel-good or rule-obeying morality? Why do you think they've fallen into this trap?

* Can you think of people whose approach to facing tough choices is an inspiration to you?

* Are there any particular times when you've felt the pain of being a finite being who can still imagine the infinite? Have you been present to other people as they've endured that pain?

2

The Search for the Honest Person

It's a famous story, hearkening back to ancient Greece. The philosopher Diogenes challenges his people to return to their roots, to embrace once again the basics of living a good life. Their lifestyle has become sophisticated—and phony. They look suave and urbane, but they're really deceitful and mean. In a word, things are a mess! So Diogenes challenges the people, urging them to abandon their foolish pretensions, to return to a simple, straightforward life of virtue, hard work, and concern for each other.

His preaching fails to convince, however. His call is rejected; and more frustrating, he's generally ignored. So Diogenes becomes more and more dramatic in making his case. At last, he's driven to a simple, prophetic gesture: Diogenes walks around, in the full light of day, carrying a lamp. It is always lit. He volunteers no word of explanation; he issues no public statement. He simply walks around the town, carrying his always-lit lamp.

"Why do you need this lamp, Diogenes?" the people finally ask him. "Can't you see just fine in the daylight?" "I cannot see what I want to see," he replies. "I am looking for one truly honest person. Until I find such a person, I shall bear my torch wherever I go."

We all do the same. We may not be as obvious as Diogenes. Even to ourselves our search may become unnoticeable, it's so much a part of who we are. When we name the critical ethical questions of our time, we may instantly gravitate to the "colorful" questions—issues of sexuality or medical technology, of international business and ethnic warfare.

But that's not all that concerns us. In those quiet, earnest conversations about the issues that trouble us personally, that we worry about when we think of raising our children or living our lives, Diogenes' concerns don't take long to appear. It soon becomes obvious that all the while we're proceeding with the activities of our lives, something else is going on, something very important even if it's also very subtle. We, like Diogenes, are walking around, carrying our metaphorical torches, desperate to find an honest person, someone we can trust.

So let's look at these less colorful, but no less important issues, the issues of honesty. Let's consider why these issues remain as troubling in our time as in Diogenes'. Let's try to name the challenges we all face in our efforts to be the kind of person that Diogenes would celebrate. Let's strategize together about how we can make our world the kind of world in which Diogenes would feel free at last to extinguish the torch in his hand.

Watch the children! Listen to them, as they play. Observe how they act and notice what they say. A pattern will quickly be revealed. You'll hear the shouted protest: "Hey, give that back! That's mine!" You'll hear the response: "No, it isn't, it's mine!" And then the inevitable appeal to authority: "Mommy, Teddy took my toy and won't give it back. Make him give it back to me. It's mine, it really is!"

Very early in life children develop this sense of possession, this realization that property belongs to a person. Of course, their first insight has to do with their own possessions: "That's mine!" They don't immediately notice the other side of the coin. But after a while it does finally dawn on them that this is a two-way street: "If this is mine, then that is yours!" Building on this, parents try to instill in their children a respect not only for their own property, but also for the property of others. They tell the children to "leave it alone," to "give it back," to "handle it with care."

If only grown-ups followed their own advice. A wise teacher once told me a wonderful story of her efforts to teach her college students about consistent honesty. At a certain point in her course, she'd open the topic of honesty and ask the students their thoughts. They'd readily declare that one should be honest and respect property rights. Then she'd give them a case to discuss. "You have friends coming to visit and you have no beer," she'd say. "Your roommate has a six-pack in the fridge. Would it be OK for you to take that beer, to offer it to your friends?"

"Sure," they'd reply. "I can always pay it back later. I'm sure my roommate would have no objection."

But then she'd switch the case. "You are the roommate. You come home after work, sweaty and tired after a rough day at your part-time job. You want nothing so much as a cool, tasty brew. But the fridge, of course, is empty. Should you be offended at this fact?"

"Of course," they'd reply, "it was my beer, not his. He should have gone out and bought his own for his guests." (Note the gender. It was the boys who got really invested in this ethical dilemma!)

My teacher friend told me it was amazing how consistently inconsistent the students were about this. Even after they'd heard the whole case and felt its impact from all sides, they found it almost impossible to embrace a consistent conclusion, that the act was either right or wrong. To the bitter end, it depended on the point of view. If they were the student with the guests, their roommate should be understanding. If they were the roommate, the host should have bought his own refreshments.

This adolescent tale may not amount to much, but it does suggest a pattern. A classroom in which I often teach looks out over a city street which, right in front of the building, takes a sharp turn. Accidents are not uncommon at that turn, especially in rainy weather. Cars roar down the street too fast, are surprised by the turn, and slide into another lane. One day, as I was teaching, exactly that happened. We heard the screech of tires and the crunch of metal. All of us, both the students and myself, turned spontaneously to look out the window. We surveyed the chaotic scene in which, luckily, no one appeared hurt. But then, suddenly, after mere seconds, one of the cars backed up, turned around, and sped away down the street in the direction from which it had come. As best I could tell from the pattern of autos, this car had caused the accident. There it was, fleeing the scene after only an instant's hesitation.

All of the students saw this, and they cried out in a single chorus. They were appalled, as I was. But there was nothing we could do, so we just stood there, filled with frustration and anger at the driver's selfishness and rank dishonesty. And we spent much of the remainder of the class discussing what all this might mean.

What it means, of course, is that we all need to take a long, courageous look at our respect for the property of others. Ironically, we have to apply to ourselves all those lessons we so easily offer to children. We have to commit ourselves once again to honoring possessions as part of honoring persons.

⟫·◦·⟪

What does it mean to be honest? It means respecting others' property, of course. But honesty also means "telling the truth." I suspect that poor old Diogenes was looking for a truthful person as much as for a person who honored others' ownership. And truthfulness is just as much of a challenge in our time.

One night, not long ago, some friends of mine were sitting on the back porch, sharing an evening's conversation.

Somehow the topic turned to "embarrassing moments." One woman's contribution moved me deeply.

"I remember one time years ago when I was caught in a bald-faced lie," she told us. "I'd made some claim or other about myself, something that reflected well on me. OK, I was bragging! And all of a sudden the facts were there for everyone to see: What I'd said was simply not the truth.

"The funny thing is that today I can't even remember the content of that lie or where I told it. I think I was so embarrassed by the experience that I've more or less repressed it. But the feeling of being caught has never left me. I was humiliated, standing before people I cared about, people whose opinions were important to me, and being revealed as someone who twists the truth. It was awful! The only good thing, I guess, is that I'm darned careful not ever to let that happen again."

This challenge of truthfulness, then, is a big part of honesty. In fact, when I listen to ordinary people complain about the moral climate of our time, one of their most bitter complaints is the way that truth has become trivialized. As I compose these lines, the newspapers are filled with examples of the verbal sparring that's become such a staple of political life, where truth seems sacrificed at a moment's notice. I'm tempted to include here examples that I've noticed, but even examples can become tools of the partisan debate. "You named his falsehoods. Why didn't you name her falsehoods?" And what really strikes me more deeply and sadly than any individual example of massaging the truth is that there's no one in public life that I feel I can trust to tell me the unembellished truth, no matter what the personal cost.

On every side, I observe self-serving distortion, willful isolation of particular details from their pertinent context, claims of candor when the ultimate objective is quite obviously to pull off a deception.

Not just politicians, either. I realize many people enjoy the Sunday morning public affairs talk shows, with guests who come from government, but also from industry, academe, even the church. I've tried to watch these shows, but I can't bear the stress. As best I can tell, everyone is trying to lie—or to "put a spin on the truth," which seems to me to be the same thing. The reporters, and sometimes the other guests, try to catch these celebrities in their lies. The winner, in the end, is not the one who tells the truth but the one who lies the best.

It's infuriating to me, and as I listen to my fellow citizens it seems just as infuriating to them. But it's also not simply a matter of our being victimized by the actions of others. What is even more troubling and what even more demands our attention just now, is the way this practice can become ours as well.

So a tough question must be asked. If Diogenes came here in search of an honest, truthful person, would I give him reason to bring his search to an end? Do I tell the truth, no matter what the personal cost? Or would my own practices suggest that I might make a wonderful politician, but that I'd offer no consolation to Diogenes on his quest?

⟫⬦⟪

The honest person tells the truth. But not all the truth. I sometimes wonder if, in our present-day culture, we've saved any sense of privacy whatsoever. It sometimes seems that the only justification some people need for a public pronouncement is the declaration that "it's the truth, after all."

Wise people through the ages described the person of true honesty as one who speaks the truth even at the price of personal disadvantage and who, at the same time, respects the privacy of others by not spreading destructive claims whether true or not. The reason, they argued, for this reticence is that for all of us the process of becoming the kind of person we want to be is slow and laborious. Mistakes are inevitably made. Those who truly wish their neighbors well, then, will allow us to learn from our mistakes. They'll honor our privacy, allowing us to leave behind our mistakes as much as possible. As long as that past behavior is no present threat to others, they will allow us to consider it dead and gone.

If we were to hold to this ancient wisdom, many things would be different in our world. For one thing, tabloid newspapers would go out of business. For the tabloids, of course, the rule is that if it's true, you can certainly publish it. (And if it's not true, then you can limit yourself to claiming that some think it might be true, and go ahead and publish it anyway!) The right to know, they argue, is the highest right. Even some of the allegedly more respectable newspapers embrace this philosophy. When challenged about some sleazy exposé or another, their defense is always "the public's right to know."

But the truth is that I do not have an unlimited right to know the affairs of others. I have the right to know what I need to know to conduct my own affairs intelligently. I have the right to know what I need to know to protect myself from danger and to make rational choices about my future. Beyond that, I have no right to know at all.

I think this is a fact that's often overlooked in our culture. Because we all have the infection of curiosity, because we simply want to know, we find it too easy to argue that we have the right to know. When I was young, it was not uncommon to hear a parent respond to a child's question: "It's none of your business." I wish we could bring back that pointed declaration.

Several years ago, Cardinal Joseph Bernardin, the Catholic bishop of Chicago, was accused of sexual behavior with an underage male. Although the young man who accused him seems to have done so sincerely—it was one of those controversial cases of repressed memory—the accusation turned out to be false. And in perhaps the most beautiful moment of the sad situation, the Cardinal and the young man, both innocent victims in their ways, were reconciled before their deaths. The most offensive moment, on the other hand, was one created by the press. Or at least I thought so.

Once the charge had been leveled against him, Cardinal Bernardin responded immediately by calling a press conference. There he told what he knew of the context, and denied any misconduct. Then he invited questions. A few questions about the exact case followed, but then the focus suddenly shifted. A reporter asked the Cardinal not about this case but, in effect, about his sexual history. "Have you ever violated your priestly vows by sexual activity?" he was asked. "Have you ever been sexually active?" Cardinal Bernardin had no choice but to answer, so he did, immediately and directly. "I have been a priest for many years. Throughout that time I have always lived a chaste and celibate life," he said.

In the whole sad episode, I was most offended that the reporter felt that question had a right to be asked. Wouldn't it be wonderful if we could learn once again to say, in circumstances where it's really appropriate: "That's none of your business"? Wouldn't it be wonderful if we ourselves, in our own settings, could learn to exercise the kind of self-control that would stop us from asking impertinent, intrusive questions?

One final thought in this regard. If it's true that, in many cases, we have no right to know at all, this is equally true of our neighbors. So if one part of honesty is not prying, another part is not telling tales. It can easily happen that we come to know the misdeeds of others, the mistakes they've made, the sins they've committed and confessed.

For that very reason it's important to remind ourselves that we have no right to broadcast these misdeeds of others just because they've somehow come to our attention. Nothing short of a genuine "need to know" justifies this sort of talk. Anything else is just tale-bearing, a polite version of character assassination.

The truly honest person says everything that's helpful, and otherwise says nothing at all.

So what shall we do, we seekers for honesty?

Scholars have studied people who performed heroic feats, showing love for others. They've looked at neighbors who ran back into the blazing building to save the last child, passersby who stopped to help the victims of a car crash, families who took in the hungry and homeless. There's even a classic study of Christian people who hid and rescued Jews during the Nazi regime in Germany. Two facts emerge from every study.

When asked, "Why did you do it?" these courageous people often plead simple luck. "Actually, I didn't know it was such a big deal, going in," they say. Isn't that often the case? At the beginning of most actions we don't know if they're a big deal or not. That kind of information only comes at the end.

Even when these people did have a sense that something important was going on, they still report that they didn't experience the choice as some sort of crisis. "I don't quite know why I did it. It was just the sort of thing we did. This way of living was in my bones, so the choice was really kind of obvious." That is, they had already established a pattern of doing the good, even at personal cost. So when the big challenge came, a habit was set and the choice was clear.

So what shall we do? When it comes to the challenges of honesty, the answer to this question is simple—not easy, but clear to anyone who will look. We have to struggle to do the good, the evident and obvious good, in all the circumstances of our life and maybe most particularly in the circumstances that don't seem important at all. For if we don't act rightly in the little deals of our lives, it will probably turn out that we won't act rightly in the big deals, either.

How about an "honesty audit"? Look back over the last week. Look, to be sure, for any moments of high drama, any times when, as it turns out, there was a big deal going on. How did you do?

But look also, maybe even more, at the little deals. Were there times when you fudged on honesty just to keep things simple, just to make things a little more convenient, just to avoid some minor awkwardness? Did you compromise someone's property rights just to get things done more quickly? Did you mask the truth to save the energy of explanation? Did you tell a shabby tale to join the group or to get a laugh or to prove your status? Well, if so, notice those times, and think about them. Raise a red flag in your mind. They are little deals, to be sure. But little deals are the turning points in the journey of the honest life.

If you discover, in your honesty audit, that you were surprisingly honest in some of those moments, then applaud yourself. Don't be shy! Congratulate yourself. Reinforce the grace of those moments. Do everything you can to turn momentary choices into lifelong habits. Like a child's blocks, each with a letter of the alphabet, let these individual moments be joined until they compose the reality called honesty.

Yes, notice the little deals, and take them seriously Because, as Diogenes knew so well, it's in undramatic choices that the stage is set for life's really tough choices.

And it's in those tough choices that the honest person is finally revealed.

Questions to Ponder

* What's been your experience regarding compromised respect for property? Have you been a victim? Have you made things worse?

* Do you think anyone tells the truth any more? In the various settings of your life, are people encouraged to tell the truth?

* Which of privacy's violations do you find more tempting, snooping or telling tales? What is it about our society that tempts us to both of these?

* Who are your heroes of respect, of candor, of discretion?

3

Sex Isn't Simple

Sex.

How can such a small, simple word represent such a complicated area of our lives?

Everyone talks about the sexual preoccupations of teenagers. With their raging hormones (and equally raging psychological needs), they seem to think of little else. When I was an adolescent, we boys thought obsession with sex was a quality of our gender. Later on I found out the girls, in their private hideouts, were just as obsessed with sex as we were, even if the exact focus of their interest might be a little different.

This preoccupation should come as no surprise. With the improved nutrition of the modern world, with vitamin-enriched bread and a year-round supply of fresh vegetables, young people achieve puberty earlier than ever. It seems they're hardly out of the crib before their periods are starting, their voices are changing, and they're running out to buy brassieres or electric razors. At the same time, young people are postponing marriage to later and later dates. There is strong pressure to get an advanced education. The expertise actually needed for most jobs and the economic pressure to keep young people out of the workforce as long as possible—both of these realities conspire to extend the time of study. And it's awfully hard to launch a successful marriage before at least one member of the couple is gainfully employed.

The result of all this is that the period between puberty and sexual commitment is not the two or three years that it was for most of human history. Rather, it's a decade or more! So the period of physical maturity without interpersonal commitment occupies a length of time unprecedented in the history of the world.

Yes, considering all these changes, as well as the barrage of sexual messages in the media, youth's focus on sex is hardly surprising.

But interest in sex is not the private preserve of adolescents. No, the power of our physical and emotional drives is a lifelong thing. A widowed uncle of mine remarried at the age of 89. I think that some of us younger relatives found this development almost disreputable, as though his needs should be any less because of his age. Thank goodness he didn't allow himself to be controlled by our preferences. Having done his best to raise his own children and to care for many others of us in the extended family, my uncle rightly felt permission to pursue his own needs in this intimate area of life. The result was that he and his new bride radiated a joy that was an inspiration to anyone willing to view it sympathetically.

No, sex isn't simple, not at the beginning and not at the end of life. Sex may be a gift, even a wondrous blessing. But sex is also a challenge that we all need to face.

Everyone knows that sex is a challenge; and as far as I can tell, sex is a challenge for everyone. But if that's true, isn't it amazing the way people keep trying to find a culprit, someone to blame for our troubles?

For some people the culprit is contemporary culture. They'll tell you that our troubles are the result of the sexual revolution. Then they'll tell you who's to blame for the revolution. All this as if our forebears in the human family didn't have their own problems with sex.

Of course, there's no doubt that we do live in a highly sexualized environment. The advertising media hit us with a constant barrage of erotic messages. It's hard to imagine how they could use sex to sell toothbrushes or lawn mowers, but they do it. And if movies are not markedly more sexually explicit today than they were years ago, certainly the advertisements for them are.

At the same time, a quick trip to the museum should be enough to remind us that artistic interest in sex is as old as the human family. Whether it's the frankly sensuous statuary of ancient Greece and Rome or the intricately erotic art of several Asian cultures, the bawdy couplets of Shakespearean plays or the voluptuous nudes of seventeenth-century European paintings, there was plenty of sex in societies far older than ours.

For other people the culprit is religion. I was raised in an Irish-American home of deeply committed Roman Catholics.

People my age have endless stories of the love affair with guilt that marked our childhood. Indeed, a psychologist friend of mine once commented that he thought he could describe a distinctive disease called "Fifties' Catholic"! And children of the sixties and seventies, even if their experience is different, still tend to believe that religion, no matter what the specific denomination, makes sex more of a problem, not less.

Maybe there's truth to this complaint against religion. But if religious traditions sometimes offer a negative, guilt-inducing vision of sex, they're also responsible for preserving and proclaiming a wonderfully healthy, wise vision of successful sexuality. I'll return to this topic near the end of the chapter, but it's worth noticing here that the common heritage of all the great religions of the world is a wonderful, life-affirming vision. In a hundred different ways they weave a three-theme tapestry: physical celebration yoked to interpersonal commitment with an eye to social generativity.

So what do you think? Is there really someone or something to blame for our troubles with sexuality? For me, the evidence of history suggests that there is no culprit. On the contrary, I think that the way sex complicates our lives is part of our very humanity.

But just because there's no culprit, it doesn't follow that there are no troubles. There are troubles galore, a range of challenges that face every one of us. Let's consider some of these challenges. And out of that let's craft a response that can help us all achieve healing and happiness.

Why is sex such a challenge for us, and where does that challenge come from? One source of the challenge we encounter in dealing with our sexuality is the simple truth that started this book, that in the human world everything costs.

I was once approached by a high school girl who asked to talk about a problem with me. The problem, it turned out, was that she was having sex with her boyfriend. Is that a problem? Actually, at first it wasn't clear to me that she thought it was. Since her relationship with her boyfriend didn't follow the conventional wisdom of the adult community, she said, she was willing to talk with me about it. But she wanted me to understand from the outset that she really didn't see any problem with it herself.

I quickly decided that listening to this young woman might prove a better strategy that arguing with her. So instead of coming up with an instant judgment of her behavior, I simply asked her why she thought having sex with her boyfriend was right. She named several reasons. She and her boyfriend had become closer as a result of their intimacy, she told me, growing in real loving concern for each other. This was giving her a joy she'd never in her life felt before. This joy, she went on, had produced a more pleasant, less grouchy attitude at home. She didn't fight with her brother and sister nearly as much as she used to. All the positive energy of this relationship had even helped her approach to school, with the result that her grades had improved and her school problems had diminished.

I listened to these statements and, as I did so, I felt a dilemma within myself. Was I really prepared to label any of these things "bad"? Was I actually going to argue that behavior with these sorts of results was nonetheless wrong? On the other hand, was I prepared to jettison the long-held wisdom of the human community, a wisdom which my own religious tradition confirms and commends? I decided to take her at her word and to respond straightforwardly to the points that she'd made.

"Well," I said, "if that's what comes of your relationship with your boyfriend, I'm not sure how I could object. After all, along with my religious tradition, I believe that acts are wrong because they harm human persons. Even the divine commands enshrined in the Bible and cherished by the Judeo-Christian tradition convey God's desire that we love one another both truly and wisely, and that we do this so that good may come of it, so that our neighbors may be truly blessed. So if your actions have these unanimously positive results, who am I to object?"

There was a long pause. She looked at me curiously, trying to decide if I was being sincere. I was, and after a moment's pause she knew it, too. So then there was a longer pause. Finally, hesitantly, softly, she spoke. "I don't want to deceive you," she said. "The situation's not absolutely perfect. Everything I've told you is true, but there's more that's also true."

"Oh really?" I asked. "How so?"

"Well, for example, it's true that I'm getting along much better with my brother and sister. But that's not everything. At home I used to be very close to my mom. I'd tell her about everything in my life. But I can't tell her about this. So I'm growing distant from her, and I'm not happy about that.

"And my two girlfriends, with whom I used to do everything, never see me any more. They're angry at me, and I miss them, too.

"Then there's the fact that my boyfriend will graduate this year and is going away to college. I'm only a junior, and when the time comes, I'll never get in the school he's attending. So I guess the truth is that our relationship is going to end. I worry about what that will be like. How will it end? And how will I feel when it's over?"

I listened to this young woman and chose my words carefully. "There's much about your relationship with this young man that's good and beautiful," I said. "But given that, and acknowledging it fully, if you had things to do over, would you do them exactly the same way next time?"

"No," she said, "I wouldn't."

—>◆<—

That young woman was experiencing one of the great truths of life, that in a finite world everything costs and nothing is absolutely perfect. She was discovering that some things are wrong not because they're utterly without merit, but because they're more destructive than necessary or because they won't, in the end, take us where we really want to go. As she was learning this truth, so I had to acknowledge this truth if I was to be really helpful to her. I had to acknowledge the complexity of her experience and this cost of which she was painfully aware.

All of us, no matter what our age, have to face that truth if we ever hope to face the challenges of sex in our lives.

I remember a wonderful movie that circulated years ago, *Lovers and Other Strangers*. A comedy, the movie had several themes. But one of the themes involved a son who comes home to his middle-aged parents, to tell them he's getting a divorce. Why? they ask. His answer is simple: Because I'm not happy.

"Happy? Happy?" asks the father. "Do you think your mother and I are happy?" And the mother pipes in, "Yes, do you think we're happy? We're not happy. We're . . ." She looks at her husband. "We're content!" he declares. And she agrees. "That's right, we're not happy, we're content."

It's a comedy, of course, so its truths are clothed in satire. But as the movie progresses, we find that these parents really are wise in their relationship. They are content—and they're happy, too. They just don't pretend that things are perfect in an imperfect world. They've accepted the costs that life imposes.

I'm not suggesting that every cost is to be accepted. We all know there are genuinely destructive relationships, where divorce is the only healthy response. But I am suggesting that many of our fellow citizens of the late twentieth century have been seduced by the illusion that perfection is possible. As a result, anything less than perfection is considered utterly unacceptable.

It may be physical perfection. I know one man who walks through life lonely, because he considers a relationship with anyone who isn't breathtakingly beautiful to be unworthy of consideration. It may be interpersonal perfection. How often, as marriages progress, do people become less and less tolerant of their partner's eccentricities? As if we didn't all have them! It may be deep-down human perfection. The scholars remind us that women and men go through the stages of adult life in different rhythms. When one partner is itching for change, the other is filled with satisfaction. And that certainly isn't perfect.

But perfection is an illusion. That, after all, is the difference between infatuation and genuine love. In infatuation, we actually think the beloved is perfect. In love, we know he or she isn't, but we love them just the same.

Yes, in a finite world everything costs. Whenever I encounter an elderly person who has lived and grown through a long-term relationship, I am struck by how they've made peace with that truth. Accepting that truth, the deeper, more exciting dimensions of sexuality have been allowed to flourish. For them, the challenge of sex has become its gift.

⟫◆⟪

Sex is a challenge. Another part of the challenge arises from the way it brings together the physical and the spiritual aspects of ourselves as persons.

I once taught a course on sexual ethics to an adult education class. On a particular day I invited the participants to complete the following sentence: "Having a body is. . . ." What a range of answers I got! "Having a body is . . . inconvenient." ". . . mildly embarrassing." ". . . great fun." ". . . work." The one thing that was clear was that having a body isn't simple.

A very wise writer, Reinhold Neibuhr, once said that human beings are a walking paradox. For human beings are both animal and angel, and by any logical standard those two things should never go together. But they do go together within each one of us. As a result, we spend our whole lives coming to grips with the paradox that we are. Because the paradox is painful and sometimes makes us feel pulled apart by contradictory impulses, said Neibuhr, we can be tempted to eliminate it, to escape from the tension by understanding ourselves as simply one or the other, either animal or angel.

My experience tells me that this insight is right. If we try to pretend we're animals alone, then we settle for lust when we should reach for love. But if we try to pretend we're angels alone, then we give in to pride when we should strive instead for compassion. Either way, we betray the mysterious paradox that we are and slide into a sort of illusion that will finally frustrate and not fulfill. Either way, we fail to respond to the challenge of our sexuality.

This was Neibuhr's insight, and he made one more important point. When human persons bail out on the paradox and settle for either angel or animal, for pride or lust, they doom themselves to failure. But of the two mistakes, the worse one, the one that is more dangerous and more destructive, is the mistake of trying to be an angel. As Neibuhr saw it, the choice to be an animal fairly quickly reveals itself as a mistake, and trying to make a life out of lust is soon seen as a dreadful error. But the choice to be an angel, building a life on a foundation of pride, is more insidious. People can go through their whole life not realizing the folly of that; and as they do so, as they live in this prideful way, they can do harm to their neighbors that no lustful person would ever even consider.

This wisdom is very important to us, as we deal with the challenge of our sexuality. We all wrestle with this paradox, after all. Some of us detach our physical urges from the anchor of our life-affirming dreams. We satisfy the urges, even as we frustrate our deeper selves, in the mistake that has long gone by the name of "lust." And that's a problem.

The destinations for people looking for mere sexual release are legion, from houses of prostitution to singles bars, from bowling alleys to country clubs. The rituals are varied, shaped by money and taste. The goals are different, too. Lust, I've always presumed, is primarily a male interest; but women tell me that, in this strange mating game, female goals are just as influential. And the results are different. Sometimes, I'm told, consensual sex is really quite harmless. I do think it's true that the wrongness of casual sex can be a matter not of its meanness but of its foolishness. But sometimes, often perhaps, it's not harmless. Indeed, it can be abusive and violent. Whether it's a matter of the gross physical violation of rape or the subtly dehumanizing moves of the party game, the wounds that are often suffered are real, and they do not quickly heal. Yes, escape into lust is a problem.

But if some of us indulge our urges in ways that are not finally fulfilling, others of us deny our physical urges altogether, pretending to a more cerebral way of life. We pretend that we don't have bodies or that embracing and appreciating these bodies is not important. We replace the embodied search for closeness with the anti-human search for control. The desire for presence degenerates into the desire for power. We become dry and cold, and settle for a "purity" that is finally sad. Indeed, we brag about it, viewing ourselves as better than those who lack such total control, and so we fall into the mistake that goes by the name of "pride."

Perhaps in our time the most obvious example of this kind of person is the celibate clergyman who takes all of the energy normally expended on the cultivation of intimate and expressive relationships, and spends that energy instead on the advancement of an ecclesiastical career. For just this reason are the central offices of various religious bodies famous for their political intrigue and interpersonal combat. All the while, these men take pride that they've never fallen victim to the lower temptations of the flesh.

But other, less obvious examples exist, too. I think of those captains of industry who are described as being married to their job. I think of university scholars who appear to live a very intellectual, almost spiritual life, but who actually are bitter and condescending snobs. And I think of Mrs. Turpin, a character in Flannery O'Connor's short story, "Resurrection." This woman has all the conventional gestures of kindness and concern. But inside, she is distant and judgmental, convinced in the depths of her heart that she's better than everyone else. She is, in her own mind's eye, an angel surrounded by animals who deserve not a thing.

One of the major challenges of our lives, then, is to resist both these temptations. We must work to weave together our bodies and our souls, affirming both, enjoying both, giving both their due. For only when we embrace this paradox at our core do we become the special reality that we are: human. Only then do we face the truth that sex isn't simple and face the challenge that it brings to every life.

What is the real challenge of sex? For adults, I think, the real challenge is not any of the points I've mentioned. Rather, it's the three-part water torture of time, tedium, and terror.

I don't know if any group ever actually used water torture, subjecting victims to a slow drip, sending them over the edge through a relentless, insidious irritant that cannot kill but also cannot be escaped. But the image strikes me as tremendously apt. When I listen to adults talk about their struggles with sexuality, their pain seems similarly relentless and insidious.

"It's time," she told me. "There are only so many hours in the day. The demands of our jobs preoccupy us. The needs of our children claim us. A thousand problems around the house and out in the neighborhood demand priority attention. Then, when a little time can finally be retrieved, we're too pooped to participate! There's just not enough time."

Or it's tedium. The old joke claims that if the newly married couple put a penny in a jar every time they have sex in the first year, then take a penny out every time they have sex after the first year is over, the jar will never be emptied. That's not my experience; still, there is a kernel of truth in the claim. In all our relationships a major hurdle is boredom. It can show itself in our ability to complete one another's sentences—and our inclination to do that. It can be revealed in the same presents, for the same holidays, year after year. It can be evident in predictable roles in sexual intimacy. It all becomes the same, so uninteresting, so predictable, and the tedium of it all robs our relationships of vitality and delight.

Or it's terror. Adults are not prone to describing their sexual feelings as terrifying, but the evidence is clear. The horrific incidence of domestic violence is the most obvious evidence of the fears that are set off in people as they begin to grow close. To be that vulnerable, to have such dependence, to find oneself so interlocked with another human being, this sort of thing scares many people to the tips of their toes. The most seriously disturbed respond to the fear through violence, physical, or psychological attack. The rest of us more typically respond through flight, abandoning the quest for genuine sexual intimacy in favor of a life lived at a safe distance from those we love the most.

Adolescents focus on the lure of physical nakedness. They imagine that the great sexual challenge is learning how to take off one's clothes without shame. They don't have a clue! The real struggle in life is achieving personal nakedness, growing comfortable in revealing ourselves to another person, feeling safe when we're stripped not of our skirts and our pants but of our roles and pretensions and disguises.

Yes, these are the grown-up challenges of sex. These are the sorts of pressures that make sex far from simple.

———❖———

Sex is a challenge, and sex just isn't simple. But that doesn't mean there's no light for us. I once presented a workshop for high school teachers who complained that they found it very difficult to talk about sexuality. They claimed that the reason for their difficulty was that they felt muzzled by the demands of authorities, people of church or community who high-jacked the classroom conversation with their personal agendas.

The complaint of the teachers may be true. But as I listened to them, it struck me that another problem was also visible. They weren't sure what they wanted to say about sex. So I spent the workshop helping them compose a script that they truly believed.

"For the next hour," I told them, "you have permission not to be a representative of your church or your school board or your town or anything else. For these minutes you have permission simply to be yourself. And to you as yourself I have a question to pose: What is it you want to tell the next generation about sex? What do you know? What has your experience taught you?" It took them a while to engage my questions, but eventually they did. When they did, beautiful things emerged.

They knew, they told me, that sex is a good and wonderful thing, one of God's great gifts, the source of much pleasure, deep warmth, joyous closeness, and beautiful care.

They knew that this good and wonderful thing seems to work best in a context of commitment, of a promised tomorrow. Sex seems to satisfy best when the partners know they can count on one another to stick around, to be there no matter what. After all, as one of the teachers pointed out, sexual release demands that one lower one's guard and risk being foolish. It's almost impossible to release oneself for sexual pleasure while still trying to be "cool." Letting go is surely much easier if one knows one's partner will not laugh—and will not leave. Commitment, these teachers wanted to say, is not the price for permissible sex, it's the home for satisfying sex.

They knew that sex draws one out of oneself and challenges one to make life. Life-making is not just the possession of those who achieve procreation, though it may be most obvious in that case. Rather, life-making more widely exists in the challenge to bond with another in the common work of loving the world. Somehow it's a dimension of all sexual encounter that it invites to a lifestyle that builds up rather than tears down, creates rather than destroys. As these teachers saw it, one of the beauties of human sexuality is the way one's sexual partner becomes one's living partner. You and I become we; and we become a force for the good of all. Through satisfying sexual expression, one way or another family comes into existence. And where family, real healthy and holy family exists, the world is truly built up.

These are the truths the teachers believed, the truths that had become clear to them in the course of their own lives, the truths they had absorbed from the best of their religious traditions. At the end of the workshop, I gave them a simple word of advice. "Don't worry about the politicized elements of the debate about sexuality. Instead, just tell your students what you know. For what you know is something they need to hear."

It's also something all of us need to hear, over and over again. Sexuality isn't simple, not for adolescents, but even more not for us adults. But it is important. So good people, people like you and me, need to speak what we have learned. And we need to believe what we have found.

If we do that, tough choices—at least in the area of human sexuality—will become wonderful moments of grace.

Questions to Ponder

- In trying to achieve sexual happiness, have you found that it's important to "accept the costs" in a finite world? Or is your experience otherwise?

- Have you encountered people who seem to be escaping the human paradox by pretending to be just angels or animals? What do you think of their efforts?

- What are your stories of time, tedium, and terror?

- What has your life taught you about sex? What would you like to tell the next generation? What do you need to tell yourself once again?

4

In the Doctors' World

I work with doctors. Every month I go to a suburban Chicago hospital that hosts a residency program in Internal Medicine. I meet with a group of the residents, discussing ethical issues that arise in their work. We deal with questions in the area usually called "medical ethics." We also talk about the professional ethics that should ground the work of physicians.

It's interesting work for me. Still, although I've been doing this work for almost five years, I can't say that I'm completely comfortable. It's not my world, and I'm not altogether at home.

When I leave my car and pass through the front door of the hospital, I leave my world. When I step into the elevator, I abandon most of the social customs by which I organize my life. When I enter the unit where I'm scheduled to meet the doctors, I enter a strange land, shaped by strange rules and guided by strange understandings. In the end, it's the doctors' world, and I am an alien visitor.

I often reflect on this, and I listen to the experiences of other people. My reaction, I find, is quite common. Indeed, it's a rare person who is comfortable dealing with medical matters. It's not just the arcane knowledge that doctors have, or our fears around the question of our health. No, it's something more subtle and sad. Whether we're going to a doctor's office for our annual physical or to an emergency room for a broken arm, we never really feel at home. In a crazy sort of way, we almost feel unwelcome. It's not our world; it's the doctors' world.

But that's not the way it should be.

"It's my body. And my body is nobody's business but my own." This line from a Broadway musical is, in its original context, a cheer for sexual liberation. As such, there's a lot that can be said against it. Still, in another sense, the declaration asserts an important truth. For it is my body; and if anyone should be in charge of its care, with authority to make decisions about its use, it should be me. In those moments when care is being taken of my body, surely I'm the one who should feel most at home, the one who should feel finally in charge.

But that's easier said than done. For lots of reasons we can feel powerless when it comes to matters of health care. To tell the truth, for lots of reasons we can choose to be powerless. If we're not careful, we can be invited to flee—can be tempted to flee—the tough choices that face us in this area. Let's try to find a better way.

⇒◆⇐

Several months ago I went to my doctor's office for my annual physical. I was the first appointment of the day, the nurse had told me, and that sounded like good news. On the other hand, this position meant I might be delayed if the doctor had emergencies at the hospital. Still, I decided to take a chance.

My choice seemed like a good one. As I hung up my coat in the waiting room, I could hear the doctor's voice coming from within. I congratulated myself on my scheduling selection. I was the first patient, and she was already in the office. Surely, things would move smoothly, efficiently, comfortably for once. But it was not to be.

For I heard the doctor's voice far more than I ever expected. I heard her make a couple of phone calls. I couldn't hear the details, of course, but it seemed she was talking to patients or to other doctors. Then I heard her discuss some medical details of a case with the colleague with whom she shared the office, as they wondered together about the interesting complexities of the case. I heard her voice as the topic of the conversation shifted to the day's headlines and to plans for vacation. I even heard her share comments with the office staff about the weather and the likelihood of rain. Indeed, I think I heard just about everything that filled the time from my scheduled appointment until I was finally invited into her office, almost a half hour late.

And she was surprised when my blood pressure reading was higher than usual!

The situation can be even worse when we're dealing with a medical crisis. I've stood at the bedside of seriously ill relatives, where I was the designated responsible person, and observed firsthand how unresponsive hospital culture can be. And the culprits were not physicians, but rather other members of the medical staff. There were exceptions, of course, caring and thoughtful practitioners of healing arts. But far too many of the staff, from nurses to lab technicians, from physical therapists to unit secretaries, telegraphed the attitude that I was an interloper in their world, an intruder they'd prefer to ignore. It's as if it were not my body—or that of the sick person—as if it was everybody's business but my own.

But that's not the case. It is my body, your body, and we can't ignore our important medical role. So as ordinary individuals we have to work at claiming our rights and accepting our responsibilities. Especially in times of crisis, it's essential that we take responsibility for the choices that are placed before us.

What does that mean? It doesn't mean being a grumpy consumer, a complainer who makes noise just to fill the air. But it does mean asking questions and expecting responses. It means making appointments, keeping appointments, and expecting appointments to be kept by others as well. It means following medical advice and cooperating in medical treatment. It means being as serious about my own health as the best of our doctors are, as responsible for my health care as the best of patients should be. It means facing the everyday struggles that my body presents to me, and responding with thoughtful decisions.

It also means facing tough choices, and facing them not in moments of crisis when the choices are thrown at us and we may be swamped by them, but now when there is no crisis and when there is time to consider and decide.

Let me tell you the story of a man I admire greatly. The story is in several chapters.

In the first chapter, he was diagnosed with cancer. He felt well and was otherwise in fine health for a person in his mid-seventies, so he asked the doctor about his options. The doctor explained that his choices included both surgery and chemotherapy. The surgery would be more risky, in the sense that this sort of assault upon the body could kill him. At the same time, if it succeeded he would have a fine chance of recovery. The chemotherapy would be less life-threatening, but it would also be accompanied by the usual unpleasant side effects. And its eventual success was questionable. In the presence of these alternatives, my friend elected surgery.

In the second chapter, after a series of recovery setbacks he finally went home from the hospital and resumed his life. He was not as vigorous as he had been; the surgery and recovery process had clearly taken their toll. But he shared time with his wife, enjoyed his friends, returned to his cherished pastime watching the golf matches on Sunday television. But then came another chapter. About two years later, symptoms led him back to his doctor. This time, after several tests a different verdict was presented: the cancer had returned, and it was now lodged in various organs of his body.

It happened that I was visiting my friend that week, so I was present in the room as the doctor explained all this to him. I must say that it was one of the finest examples of good doctoring that I've ever seen. The doctor was gentle but clear. He explained that this time, too, there were two options. Chemotherapy was possible. However, in cases such as this, the therapy was known to achieve some positive effect in only a third of the cases. Even in those cases, it would not remove the disease; it would only add a few months to his life. And, of course, there would be the unpleasant side effects. The other option, explained the doctor, would be to forgo the therapy and instead begin a plan of "comfort care," allowing him to enjoy his limited life expectancy in the company of his wife and friends. Finally, the doctor urged him to take a few days' time to reach his decision and to feel completely free to go either way.

It was a sad moment, to be sure. But it was also beautiful in its way. My friend said he would follow the doctor's advice and think about it for a few days before he made a firm decision. But he also wanted the doctor to know that his immediate thought was to skip the chemotherapy. "We all have to die, after all," he said. "I would much rather be comfortable and able to share with my family than be distracted by the therapy process." At last, after my friend had spoken his mind, the doctor shared his. "I'll do whatever you want," he said. "But to be honest, the choice you're considering is the choice I'd make, too."

My friend died in a setting of love and gentle care. And I was filled with admiration for him, for his doctor, and for the family that surrounded him. He was not shy about using the wonders of modern medicine when they offered reasonable expectation of helping him live a happy and involved life. But he didn't see mere survival as the highest priority. His benchmark for success was not existence but relationship. He was able to make good choices because he'd accepted the most often denied fact of our world: that he would someday die.

In recent decades, people who think about the ethics of medical care have highlighted the notion of autonomy, the idea that individuals have a right to make key decisions in their own health care. As I've mentioned, the medical system isn't always very sensitive to patient autonomy. But at least in principle, everyone acknowledges its reality.

As a support to the autonomy of the patient, procedures have been created that allow people to provide "advance directives" indicating what sort of care they prefer: aggressive, survive-at-all-costs initiatives, or reasonable-efforts-and-then-comfort-care approaches. In fact, procedures for formulating and communicating these advance directives have been in place for some years.

After all the years of their existence, however, the scary truth is that most people haven't prepared any advanced directives. People are not willing, it would seem, to face the reality of their own death or to imagine the sorts of tough choices that may have to be made. So in most cases, even those doctors who would conscientiously follow the wishes of autonomous patients have no guidelines to follow.

So here's the first tough choice we all face. It's the choice whether to acknowledge our own mortality or not. It's a flippant comment, but a profound truth, that no one gets out of life alive! It's also a truth so easily denied, or at least so successfully circumvented. To face our tough choices in the doctors' world, we have to do better.

What about you, then? Do you ever talk about your death? With those you love, your spouse or your children, do you talk about your vision of life and your understanding of death? Have you considered your vision of how life should end, whether in a hospital-based high-tech battle or in a home-based circle of care? Have you explored these questions, calmly and in a time of health? Having talked about them, have you shared your wisdom about all this?

Have you discussed these medical preferences with your doctor? I realize that in this age of managed care many people don't have the luxury of an ongoing relationship with a particular doctor. So it's not easy to get your wishes recognized and recorded. But if your circumstances allow it, this topic is certainly worth an early and everyday conversation.

The residents with whom I work each month struggle almost daily with conversations about individual choice. As they do so, they feel the terrible frustration that the conversation is taking place too late. This reflection on the kind of treatment we want should almost always take place before we are in the hospital. It should be part of a physical exam, when it's much less anxiety-provoking.

A fascinating study found that the strongest predictor of people's satisfaction with their doctor's care wasn't the doctor's medical training, or even the doctor's personality. It was a harmony between the doctor's overall view of life and the patient's. So this conversation that produces advance directives is a two-way street. As patients we should describe the kind of care we want. As patients we should also ask our doctor about the kind of care she or he prefers to give.

What are your advanced directives? I don't mean the piece of paper, I mean your actual wishes. And if you don't have any, now might be a fine time to begin to make a change. Now might be a fine time to face this tough choice.

⋙⋅◆⋅⋘

Then there's the story of a friend of mine who, several years ago, was confronted with her father's mortality. The father had experienced various health problems over the years, but he had continued to function, to relate and to enjoy life. Then he had a stroke, which resulted in his being placed on a ventilator. Much of the time he was somewhat conscious and seemed able to recognize his wife and some other people. But he couldn't move, and it was unclear whether he was really in communication with those around him.

Eventually, the man had to be moved from the regular hospital to a facility that specialized in caring for people on ventilators. There he remained for the better part of a year. On several occasions his situation would deteriorate. He'd get pneumonia or seem to suffer a small additional stroke. But then he'd rally, returning to this semi-conscious, minimally communicative plateau.

Situations like this are very complicated, of course. For one thing, in the presence of even a slight ability to communicate, many would argue that no one should make life and death decisions but the man himself. For another, there are many different ways of responding to situations like this. In any case, that's not my focus here. What I watched with sadness through these months—and what I want to describe—was the behavior of this man's family.

At one point the doctor asked the man's wife if he should enter a "DNR" order, so that, if he should suffer a heart attack, the instruction to the staff would be "do not resuscitate." "No," said his wife, "don't do that. I want you to resuscitate him so that I can be there when he dies."

At several other points, the family had conversations in which they offered opinions about how things might go. One daughter, my friend, accepted the candid judgment of the doctor that this man would not improve and would die within months. But the other daughter, against all the evidence, continued to expect her father's complete recovery; and, of course, in service to that end, she expected the medical staff to pursue all aggressive interventions.

64

What was clear in this family was that old and complicated issues were cluttering this moment of crisis. Guilt over past negligence was prompting people to make extravagant commitments, as if they could now prove the love that they'd failed to show in the past. And personal needs of various members of the family were taking precedence over judgments about what was best for the dying man, indeed were leading family members to demand that this man continue to live, for their sake far more than for his.

A famous researcher, Elizabeth Kubler-Ross, has shown that the process of dying is profoundly interpersonal and, in some mysterious ways, quite free. People with a terminal illness tend to die when and how they want. They tend not to die until their "work is finished," and they often die quite quickly once matters have been resolved and goals have been met. This research leads me to ask why this man was not dying. My suspicion is that he was not dying because he had not been given permission to die. I think he sensed the resistance on the part of some family members to his own dying process. His wife in particular was, in some subtle but real way, demanding that he continue to live for her. Because he loved her, he was trying very hard to do exactly that.

The challenge for this family was to accept the truth that their husband and father must die, as we all must die. If it was his wish to live at all costs, then they should surely work to support him in that wish. But what if that was not his wish? What if he had come to grips with his inevitable death and was willing to embrace that final act of living that is our dying? I believe they should support that as well. They should communicate to this man that they're willing to let him go, that they will be present to him both in his living and in his dying. They should make the painful but crucial decision to meet their needs some other way and to set this poor man free.

———◆———

I don't know all the inner details of this family's life, of course. The story that I tell is part my fabrication, since it combines my observations of their actions with my own speculations about their motives. So I can't tell you exactly what they each did, or why they did it. What I can tell you is that the man did eventually die and that the family felt a peace and acceptance when his death finally occurred.

And I can tell you that the issues they faced are issues all of us must someday face. In fact, these issues present us with another tough choice that we all must make.

My experience is that times of sickness and dying bring out the best and the worst in families. The doctors with whom I work confirm this. I've spoken about the tendency of the medical establishment to overlook patient autonomy, to focus on their own scientific agenda instead of the broader human agenda of persons who must both live and die. But if that's sometimes true, it's also often true that doctors who work to keep this broader perspective find themselves thwarted by the families who are nearby.

We can stop that. We can take this story as a lesson, and seek to apply it in the varied circumstances of our lives. In this complicated world of ours, where so many values conflict and so many actions cost more than we'd like, we can try to reach decisions that express true love, faithful and also freeing, courageous and also comforting.

We can face the tough choice that life presents us here: to accept the mortality of others as truly as we accept our own. In some ways this is the more difficult choice. It's one thing to accept that I must die. It's another thing, in so many ways a more difficult thing, to accept that those I love must die. Have you forced yourself to realize that no one except God can take care of you forever? Have you agreed to live in the presence of that painful truth? Have you embraced the everyday struggle to enjoy the love of others while also acknowledging that the comforts of this love must someday be finally relinquished?

Have you faced what may be the most painful truth of all, that we all fail one another at some times and in some ways and that when death comes, we will all have some regrets? This can't be avoided, and the time of dying must not be used as a vain attempt to set the scales aright. Or maybe better, the only way dying can be used to set the scales aright is by the truly courageous act of love involved in letting the other person go.

⇒◆⇐

There are many lessons to be learned in the doctors' world. There's the lesson of our ongoing responsibility for our regular health care. In situations where it's easy to be intimidated, it takes work to remember that it's "my body." It takes effort to ask questions, express concerns, make reasonable demands, understand reasonable limits, offer reasonable cooperation. It takes courage to accept responsibility when that also involves claiming authority, especially when the system may too easily overlook that authority. But it's an important lesson nonetheless.

There's the lesson of our own mortality. It takes tremendous honesty to talk about things that are hard to talk about, to raise issues that are frightening to contemplate. It takes gentleness to open this topic with those we love. It takes patience to open it with medical personnel who may be even more uncomfortable than we are.

There's the lesson of the mortality of those we love. Of course, part of this lesson is to treat people each day in a way that will leave no regrets when they die. But that's easier said than done. So another part of the lesson is the admission that none of us is perfect and no life is without regrets. The lesson is a challenge to love others with a freeing love, when that is probably the hardest thing that can be done. As a woman once beautifully put it to me in talking about her husband, "I'd much rather he live. But if he must live the way he is now, in pain and without communication, I'd rather allow him to die. I love him too much to extend his useless pain."

These are the lessons that are offered us all, the challenges that face us all, as we face ourselves in this so-called "doctors' world." It's not their world, of course. It's our world, with tough choices that are finally ours to make. For the choices are about our lives, and no one else's.

As this life has been placed in our hands by a loving God, so it must be cherished lovingly, carried responsibly, and, when the moment comes, given back with gentle trust.

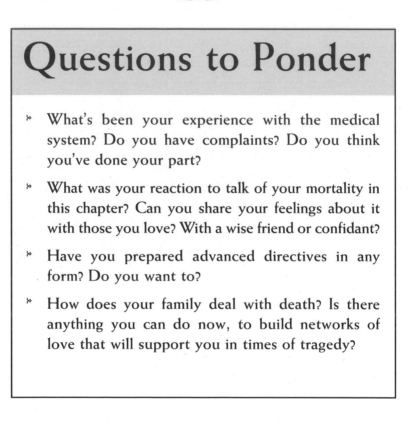

Questions to Ponder

❧ What's been your experience with the medical system? Do you have complaints? Do you think you've done your part?

❧ What was your reaction to talk of your mortality in this chapter? Can you share your feelings about it with those you love? With a wise friend or confidant?

❧ Have you prepared advanced directives in any form? Do you want to?

❧ How does your family deal with death? Is there anything you can do now, to build networks of love that will support you in times of tragedy?

5

It's Only a Job

Yesterday, the phone rang just as we were about to sit down to dinner. I answered it. There was that telling pause of a second or two before a live voice, a woman's voice, cheery and friendly, came on the line. "May I speak to Timothy O'Connell?" Perhaps I should have said: "Who? No one by that name here!" But I didn't. Instead, I answered truthfully: "Speaking."

"Congratulations, Mr. O'Connell. You have been pre-approved for an XYZ credit card, and we're sending it right out to you!"

"Oh, no, you're not!" I snapped. "I don't want your card. I do want any account you've created to be cancelled. And any card I receive, I'll destroy."

After the briefest of pauses, she replied, "Thank you for your time. Have a nice day." And she hung up.

I've thought of that woman several times since the telephone call. In our very brief conversation, she seemed like a nice enough person. Certainly, she'd been trained by her supervisor to be polite, and she made no real attempt to bully me.

At the same time, her "pitch" was innately manipulative. Her script made it sound as if this was a great honor I'd received. It gave the impression that we were talking about a genuine gift, rather than a way of making money off of me. So I find myself thinking of her.

What does she think of her job? Does she have a sense of having abandoned her integrity in accepting this task? Every time a person picks up the phone at the other end, does she flinch at the carefully honed speech she must now present? Does she accept any responsibility for the actions of the person on the other end of the line? Or is she so desperate for work that she'll allow no scruples of conscience? Is it, once again, a matter of "buyer beware"?

Here is an idea we often flee. Our character is expressed in our work perhaps more clearly than in any other sector of our lives. Nowhere else are there likely to be so many moral dilemmas. Nowhere else are the challenges to good people so constant. Talk about tough choices? That's another name for a job!

But I'll bet you knew that already!

⟫⟪

Where are the dilemmas in your job?

I know a man, Karl's his name, who put in thirty hard years on the assembly line of a manufacturing firm. Then his job was eliminated, and in his mid-fifties he was looking for work. A casual buddy alerted him to a job as a night-time security guard in a motorcycle factory. Karl took the job. The money was OK; and, to tell the truth, wandering around all night looking at motorcycles sounded like fun. It was fun, at least until he discovered that his buddy was stealing parts from the factory. Now, what's Karl supposed to do?

Then there's Nola. She's the financial director for an investment firm. It's a small firm, privately owned. But the founder has delegated most of his authority to a board of directors, since he no longer wants to be involved in the venture day in and day out. Now, with disconcerting regularity Nola has to deal with a certain director. He's an active alcoholic who misunderstands many of the issues, sleeps through parts of the meetings, and, when he's awake, peppers his haughty comments with offensive sexual innuendos. Even between meetings, she can't avoid him. She has to take his phone calls at unexpected moments, spend time crafting letters of response to his hastily scribbled memos, smile genially when he shows up in the office unannounced and generously lubricated. Not coincidentally, this director is the founder's brother-in-law!

Denny is an energetic and creative type, destined to be an entrepreneur. He's bright, and he works hard. He's also a man of integrity. So when he started a small manufacturing company, Denny committed himself to obeying all the environmental laws. After all, it's not only the law, it's also in the best interest of our health. His competitors, sad to say, weren't so conscientious. They found sneaky ways to hide their pollution, to get rid of their waste without cleaning it up, to avoid the costs that would come from obeying the spirit as well as the letter of these laws. After a long struggle, Denny finally resigned himself to the painful truth, that he couldn't compete successfully in an industry where others routinely cheated and he did not. He abandoned his project.

And there's Lois. She's always had a tough time. She never finished high school; and she's always worked at least part-time, even while raising her family. Now the kids are grown. Back to work full-time, Lois gets a job as a housekeeper in a local hotel. They're really rather nice, explaining how she can take periodic breaks and showing her the break room. Slowly, it dawns on her. Almost all the other housekeepers are minority women. They're never in the break room. Truth is, they aren't welcome, and they know it. Lois doesn't feel good.

Finally, there's Alice, a young woman who's just getting started, a small job in a large company. Alice is the assistant to a middle manager, and it's clear that her own future in the company is linked to the manager's future. After all, he hired her, and if he wants to he can replace her. The problem, however, is that the manager is untrustworthy. Alice has watched him falsify expense reports, make promises to customers that he knew he couldn't keep, respond with bald-faced lies to questions from the company's top management. In the midst of all this, Alice feels trapped, for if she reports her boss, one of two things will happen.

One possibility is that Alice won't be believed, that her boss will come up with some quick-witted explanation that will satisfy the company leaders. If that happens, of course, her days in this job are numbered. The other possibility is that she will be believed and her boss will be out on his ear. She may even get a gesture of thanks from the people at the top. But if all this happens, the end result will probably be that someone else will take her boss's job, and that person will probably decide to bring in his or her own assistants. The result: her days will still be numbered! The frustration is almost more than Alice can bear.

What about you? What are the frustrations that plague you in your job? Is the problem the boss? Or the customer? Or the colleague? Or the industry? Or the competition? Or the whole darned situation?

It's so tough to work and to keep your honor. But maybe we can bring to light some ideas that may make it just a little bit easier. Maybe we can find a way to make this part of our lives something more than "just a job." Maybe we can actually join honor to success, at least part of the time and part of the way.

It's worth a try.

The Bible's Book of Genesis is a prized source for several of the world's great religions. One of the most well-known stories from that book is the tale of the sin of Adam and Eve. You know the story, filled as it is with wonderful poetry, metaphors, and images that point to deep, amazingly relevant truths.

Adam and Eve live in a place of perfection, where everything is possible. Their environment is filled with attractive and useful things, only one of which is prohibited to them. The Bible calls it the fruit of the tree of the knowledge of good and evil. You can't help asking, "Why is that fruit forbidden?" Though many people have interesting answers to that question, they really don't make any difference. The point of the story is simply that something ought not to be done, but they do it anyway. And the result of doing what ought not to be done? Everything unravels. Adam and Eve lose their innocence in unavoidable shame. They lose their loving relationship in mutual recriminations. They lose their peaceful and comfortable situation in their sense of embarrassed discomfort. In the end, there's really no choice but to leave.

Scholars call the reality presented in this wondrous story "original sin," and by this term they mean two things. On the one hand, they mean a bad choice that sets everything wrong, a mistake that causes the whole situation to unravel. On the other hand, they mean the messes in which we're all mired, situations that sometimes result from bad decisions, even decisions made long ago and far away, and that just cannot be undone.

I can identify both these senses of original sin in my own life. There are times when I've done something stupid or mean, and the result was that everything came undone. There are also times when I've found myself caught in a web of destructiveness; it was very difficult to say who was to blame, but the force for harm was very real nonetheless. I'd imagine that you can locate the same sorts of experiences.

When I was young, filled with energy and enthusiasm, a very wise old woman once told me, "Don't take your present virtue for granted. Original sin is the 'noon-day devil.' It's the weight of fatigue that leads us, little by little, away from the ideals of our youth." As I've gotten older, I've discovered that this insightful woman was right. Most of us don't reject our ideals with a vengeance. Rather, we slip away from them, ever so slowly, filling in the space with pragmatism and with conventionality.

At the beginning, we have inner commitment, a vision of the kind of person we want to be and a plan for the kind of behaviors that will lead us in the right direction. We see our job as more than a job, as a career, maybe even a vocation, a way to contribute to the world at the same time as we make a living for ourselves and for those we love. But then, in the rush of everyday activity, the inner vision starts to lose its force.

It's not that we start to do bad things right away. It's just that, while we happen to do good things, it becomes less and less important to us that we do them. For it's one of the curiosities of human persons that we're able to stick with upright behaviors long after they lose their grounding in genuine commitment to the good, acting the part of the virtuous person even as the desire for true virtue wanes. We "surface out" in terms of our dream of life, so that good and honest behavior becomes more and more a simple convention and less and less a true commitment.

Then comes the moment of challenge, when someone offers us some large advantage if we lie or steal or cheat. Since our good actions are no longer rooted in serious, intentional commitment, since they're more habit than wholehearted, they are quite easy to abandon. We wake up some morning, then, surprised with ourselves. We've become someone we hadn't planned to be. Our principles are gone, our good actions are a thing of the past. There's no longer any way to deny it. We are out for Number One, and ready to hurt anyone who gets in the way.

It's a sad story, and frightening as well. Commitment slides into mere conventionality; then challenge results in collapse. But it's, oh, so true. And it's, oh, so common. It is, truth to tell, the original sin we do and that does us in.

———⊰•⊱———

I've described in these pages the work I do occasionally, helping medical residents to reflect on the ethical issues of their situation. When I accepted this part-time position, my original job description called for me to spend my time discussing issues in medical ethics with these residents, considering the relative merits of various medical alternatives in light of the needs and wants of the patients who were involved. But as we've grown more comfortable with each other, the doctors and I, I find that they spend much of our time together pursuing not medical ethics but professional ethics. That is, the dilemmas they want to discuss have more to do with issues of upright behavior among doctors than with questions of upright service to the patients. This has surprised me very much.

My residents tell me of their frustrations in dealing with some of the attending physicians, those doctors in private practice who admit patients to this hospital. The residents are convinced that they see cases where the length of stay in the hospital and the number of tests taken is determined not by the medical needs of the patient but by the level of insurance available to pay for it all. Sometimes, in the most offensive cases, they believe they witness doctors refusing to pursue appropriate avenues of care because a patient doesn't have insurance. Much more commonly, they believe, they see a multiplication of tests and an extension of stay in cases where insurance won't protest.

The residents object to all this. From the perspective of their youthful idealism they look at all these behaviors and they find them repugnant. But I can tell they're also asking a quiet, fearful question: "Will this be me one day?"

It could be. The noon-day devil can besiege the best of us. I imagine you encounter it frequently.

Is there anything more contradictory than a grumpy and argumentative clergy person? Yet one sees it, or hears of it, all the time. A minister limits his availability or cuts short her presence at meetings, delivers sermons written on the back of an envelope in scribbled notes that even the speaker can't read! Haughtiness replaces humility. Energy is spent serving self instead of serving others. The client becomes the enemy. The parishioner is treated as a pest. We see the idealism of youth give way to the indolence of a tired mid-life.

Yes, the noon-day devil can affect all of us. The other day I was in the grocery store. Just ahead of me, the cashier asked a customer if she had a membership card for this particular chain of stores. But the question was asked in such a mumbled undertone that the customer couldn't understand it. Several times, she indicated she didn't understand. The cashier repeated the question, but the mumbling was no more intelligible. I couldn't decide whether the woman at the cash register meant to be mean, or whether what I was seeing was simply personal thoughtlessness combined with a lack of training. But the result was certainly an unpleasant experience, and it was obvious that the customer felt embarrassed and demeaned.

I'm astonished at the frequency with which I see this kind of thing. I go into a store, ask the attendant for help or service, and receive instead the unmistakable message that the assistance I'm receiving is a favor for which I should be grateful in the extreme. Actually, I thought I was the one doing the favor by patronizing the store. But that's certainly not the perspective of these staff. They find my presence inconvenient, or so it seems.

That noon-day devil, we encounter it wherever we go. It's not hard to imagine that it really is the original sin, a root of all evil that poisons the well from which we all drink.

⫸◆⫷

I've long watched the way people behave in their jobs. I've watched myself, as well. I suspect that nothing explains the moral dilemmas that confront us in the working world as well as this ancient idea of original sin, the mess that is bigger than us all.

Oh, I know that there are cases of genuine meanness to be found, there are people who are not hesitant about plundering the world and bruising the neighbor and hogging the wealth. Every one of us can tell stories of people like this, and we can verify the way they pollute the whole situation and ruin what could otherwise be beautiful by their acts. But it's much more common, I think, that good people just run out of steam.

If that's true, then an important lesson has been presented to us. For you and me, the kind of people who read books like this (and who write them, I hope), are good people. If we'd settled willingly and firmly into a life of selfish dishonor, we wouldn't be wasting our time with the tough choices these pages describe. But we haven't. We set out upon the journey of our lives with a desire to be good and to do good. To a very significant degree, we continue to dream of that way of life. So we look for insight and inspiration, in order to persevere in trying to live that dream. We turn to these pages, looking for ideas that may help, examples that may illumine, suggestions that may assist.

Here is one suggestion that's important: beware the noonday devil. Beware of fatigue. Beware of forgetfulness and apathy and exhaustion. And do whatever is necessary to resist these tokens of original sin.

Keep the dream alive. Toward that end, talk about the dream, find kindred spirits and share the dream among you. Dreams that aren't shared don't survive, and dreams flourish in the soil of sharing. Find ways to reward yourself for persevering in the dream. Don't try to deny that serving the dream has a cost.

At the least honor that cost by naming it, and try to compensate for it in some other area of your life. And face the painful fact that some settings may be hopelessly toxic to the dream, that you may need to abandon some paths, move out and move along, if the dream is to stay alive.

It's not, after all, just a job. It's your life, spilt out on the altar of daily labor, spent so that, at one and the same time, rewards can come to you and yours and the world can become a somewhat better place. It's not just a job. And it's certainly, at its heart, not part of original sin.

Quite the contrary, as wise philosophers have always known, this work, this creativity, this contribution, this service, this effort of yours is original blessing, a grace to humans in a truly human world.

Questions to Ponder

» Have you seen evidence of the "noon-day devil," little by little losing the commitment with which we began? Have you observed it in others? Felt it in yourself?

» Have you encountered any terrible examples of people who have lost their character through their job?

» What are the tough choices of your job? Have they always been the same, or have they changed over time?

» Do you have any heroes who show you that it's possible to be a person of character in one's job?

6

Show Me the Money

All marriage counselors tell the same story. Here's how Adelaide put it:

"People presume that the greatest challenge facing newly-weds is in the area of sex. Finding sexual compatibility, accommodating to each other's sexual needs and desires—surely this is the greatest adjustment for those entering the married state. But it's not so. The greatest area of difficulty is money! It's money that starts most of the fights. It's money that causes most of the conflict. It's money that disrupts and undermines the relationship."

It is so easy to overlook the importance of money in our lives. I don't mean that we ever forget the bald fact that money is important. Of course it is. But I do mean that we often underestimate the power money has over us, the way it can twist our minds and change our priorities.

I recently attended the funeral of an elderly man, the grandfather of a friend of mine. During the luncheon after the funeral I began to sense tension among some of the family members. Down at the far end of the table, one of the grandchildren was keeping to herself; it almost seemed as if she was pouting.

Then, a couple of times, I would catch a couple of the grandchildren whispering among themselves.

When a quiet moment came, I finally had a chance to ask my friend for an explanation. I asked her if she'd noticed the tension, and the whispers. "Oh yes," she said. "I did. And I know what's going on. Sylvia's angry," she told me, referring to her sister. "She just found out that Grandpa left his TV to the nurse who took care of him. The last thing Sylvia needs is another TV. But she's still furious that anyone outside the family got it. She thinks Mom should have overruled Grandpa's wishes and kept the TV for us."

As you probably know already, stories like this are very common. I know of one family in which the father, a widower, had remarried shortly before his death. The new wife gave him tremendous joy in his final year, and it was obvious that the father never regretted his choice. Still, the grown children resented the fact that, when their father died, his new wife, now his widow, was legally entitled to a major share of his estate. In all honesty, the children were all quite well-off; they didn't need the money. Nonetheless, it really angered them that this income was going to someone else and not to them. Yes, stories like this are found in every community.

They're even found in religious scriptures. The Christian gospels include the wonderful parable of the landowner who paid last-minute workers a full day's pay. Then when he finally got around to paying those who had worked all day, they expected to get more, even though they had already agreed to a particular sum.

The landowner's striking response has echoed through the centuries: "Are you envious because I am generous?" (Matthew 20:1–15).

—————

Yes, money holds a terrible power over us. It can make us do things we never imagined, lead us to violate principles we thought we held dear. Why is that?

I suppose there are many reasons for money's power over us. But certainly part of the reason is that money, in and of itself, has power. Money can get us things we want. Often it's not the money itself we covet; it's the things that money can buy. Money can bring us comfort, entertainment, pleasure, beauty, security, perhaps even a longer life. And we want these things. We want to travel, we want to enjoy, we want to experience, we want to possess, we want to live. Because money can bring us these things we want, money has power—power in itself and power over us.

To some extent (though we often deny it) money can even get us people. Money can make us more attractive to others, lead others to want to be around us. At the very least, money can make it possible for us to be in places and to do things that will call us to the attention of others. That attention may lead others to decide they want us as friends, perhaps even as a spouse.

I remember a conversation I had more than twenty years ago. I was talking with a man I greatly admired, a person who was something of a mentor to me. We were talking about his work and why he enjoyed it. Suddenly, he offered an observation that stunned and troubled me and has remained with me ever since. "Let's face it, Tim," he said. "Rich people are usually more interesting."

I don't know if this man meant that rich people are interesting because they're rich, or that interesting people are more likely to become rich, or even that riches allow people to do things that are interesting and that make them interesting. But in any case, I was really shaken by the coldness and finality of his statement. It somehow felt to me that if what he said were true, and if we were to decide to live on the basis of this judgment, the results could be very bad. At the least, the results would be very sad.

Here's the issue. Money has power over us, but it's a power that can be either for good or for ill. On the one hand, as the wise saying has it, "money is the root of all evil." On the other hand, money does provide a power for good, equipping people of good heart with the wherewithal to make wonderful things happen in our world. So money can lead us either way, toward love and care, responsibility and concern, or toward selfishness and disinterest, violence and deceit.

Either way, then, money is a moral issue. It's a place where very important tough choices take place. Money matters are matters where we often feel "caught." So, let's share some more stories of money. And let's see if we can find wisdom that will help resolve the dilemmas that money so regularly presents.

⇒◆⇐

For years I've worked with young people. As I've worked with them and watched them, I've often tried to discern the exact moment at which they decide they're no longer children, but now adults It's often hard to tell when that moment arrives. After all, the process of growing up is complicated, and it continues over a long period of time. But I do think a moment comes when these people decide they are adults and begin acting according to the rules and expectations that adults accept. And I think that one major indicator of this entrance into adulthood—or into an adult identity—is that the young person starts to share money with those less fortunate.

Go to the church services that take place on college campuses, for example. Or even look around at your own place of worship. When the basket is passed, do you see the children contributing? Oh, I know that in some families Mom and Dad slip some coins into the hands of their children so that they, too, will have the experience of giving. And I think that's a wonderful practice. But that's not what I'm talking about. I'm asking whether the young people freely give from their own resources, digging into their own pockets to find something to put in the collection basket.

Of course, the answer to my question is obvious. You won't see the youngsters contributing. Why not? Are they mean and selfish persons? I don't think so, and in many ways their behavior says just the opposite about them. If you ask young people to contribute time or talent to some worthy cause or other, they're usually more than willing to oblige. In fact, they seem happy to be able to help. But when it comes to contributing in a

89

financial way to causes, it's something else altogether. Is it simply that they're broke, that they have no money of their own? No, I don't think that's the reason, either. After all, they find the money to go on a date, to buy a CD, to give a birthday present to a friend.

No, I think the reason why young people don't donate is simply that they don't think it's their job. I think their failure to contribute comes from a presumption, deep in their hearts even if it's actually unconsidered, that donating is "something the grown-ups do." In their understanding of themselves, these young people are still on the receiving end of grown-up largesse. They take it, they don't give it. And since, at least in this regard, they don't imagine themselves as grown-ups, they also don't participate in the grown-up activity of sharing their wealth with others.

I had a somewhat pointed conversation about all this several years ago when I shared a holiday with a group of friends and relatives. The conversation had come to focus on the young people in the group. Two of the young people had brought along a date, in each case someone they'd only recently started seeing. So, at one point in the after-dinner conversation, the adults started a friendly grilling of these dates, inquiring—to the amusement of the other young people—about their plans and dreams, even about their grades in school. Both of the new dates answered well. I think they felt some pride in weathering the conversation, and they received warm affirmation from the adults. In fact, several of us went out of our way to encourage the young people to continue their education, to develop their skills and, in various ways, to persevere in pursuing their dreams of great achievement.

But then the conversation shifted. One of the relatives, a young man, said he was bothered by all these questions and by our comments. Why should these people have dreams and plans? Why should they have to "do something" with their lives? Why couldn't they just be? After all, that was his approach. He had finished high school, had decided not to pursue any further education, and instead had gotten a job. He was happy just as he was. He was satisfied with his salary, enjoyed his life, and had no ambitions of change or growth or development. In fact, except for his desire to get married some day, he really didn't "have any plans." And why should he? (It was interesting that the young woman he was dating and with whom he might well enter marriage, did not go out of her way to applaud this position!)

I couldn't resist challenging the young man. "Well, then," I said, "it seems as if you're saying that you are fully an adult. You aren't some kind of adolescent, building for a future that you hope to achieve. Rather, you're a grown-up, occupying the position you want and living the life you choose."

"That's right," he responded.

"If that's so," I continued, "how much do you give to charity? Grown-ups give to charity. Adolescents don't, I realize. After all, they're using their money to develop themselves so that they can later make a greater contribution to those they love and to society. But you say that you aren't an adolescent, that you're a grown-up. If that's so, then as a grown-up you should be sharing your wealth. So, how much do you give to charity?"

You can guess his answer. He gave nothing. At first, he tried to challenge the assumption underneath my question, that grown-ups share with those less fortunate, by arguing that the poor don't deserve our help. Actually, I hadn't said anything about "giving to the poor," but I let that pass. "OK," I said. "You don't think the homeless deserve your money, or the hungry. What about the American Cancer Society or the Red Cross? Surely these organizations do good work. Why not help them?"

He didn't really have an answer, and I quickly changed the subject since I didn't want to embarrass him. But I did want to get him thinking. I wanted to offer the possibility that his claims of adulthood weren't as well-founded as he thought. In many ways, this young man really had yet to imagine himself as a "citizen," as an adult, as a person who shares with those less fortunate. In his own mind, despite his protests, he was still an adolescent, still on the dole.

He had some more growing to do. And maybe we do, too, no matter what our chronological age.

———◆———

One of the signs of being a grown-up is that we share our wealth with those less fortunate. Or is that really true? After all, the questions I put to this adolescent could just as easily be put to many of us who are much older. How do we come to a good attitude about money? I think the starting point for a good attitude about money is the realization that we have all been astonishingly gifted.

Some years ago I taught a young man, a very impressive individual. He was very bright, and he was also hard-working. He had goals for his life and he was serious about pursuing those goals. In lots of ways this young man was someone to admire.

But he was also a little infuriating. On more than one occasion I heard him express the opinion that, in life, everyone needs to take care of themselves. We can't depend on others, and we have no responsibility to let others depend on us. After all, he'd say, everything that he had accomplished had been his own doing. No one had taken care of him. So he had no intention of taking care of anyone else. It was everyone for themselves.

How ridiculous, I thought! As if I didn't know his life story! This young man came from a family of bright and productive people. Habits of hard work and the talent to achieve had been part of his family fabric for generations. Indeed, though I know it irritated him to admit it, the fact was that much of his talent had been genetically predetermined, a gift he hadn't requested and hadn't particularly deserved.

What's more, he had been raised in a stable home, with excellent nutrition and endless stimulation. Family conversations had honed his mind, developed his understandings, expanded his vocabulary, deepened his self-confidence. Then, as if all that hadn't been enough, his family was sufficiently wealthy that his parents were able to bankroll his education at a prestigious college. No part-time job for him, no need to squeeze in studying between hours of numbing work. No, he was able to "enjoy" his education, if that term is ever really accurate.

I don't deny that this young man worked at his own development. After all, no one passed the exams but him. So I didn't ask that he have no pride in his accomplishments. I just wished he would admit that he had built on foundations provided by others, that his accomplishments had been grown from seeds that were nothing but gifts.

I'm happy to report that he does now admit this. In due course, he met and fell in love with a lovely young woman, a person of gentleness and sensitivity. For a while their affection for each other grew without much struggle. But then a crisis occurred: she just couldn't abide his blindness to his gifts. At one point, she actually told him so. "I'm sad to say this, but the truth is I don't like you very much. I like so much about you. But the 'you' at the center, that's something I don't like. I don't think I want to be around you."

A conversion came from this confrontation. His eyes were opened. These two young people are now married, and I've come to admire them both, as they bring out the best in each other. I can now sense a wonderful balance in their attitudes. On the one hand, they're proud of what they've achieved, as well they should be. On the other hand, they're acutely aware of how blessed they've been along the way, how lucky in the gamble of life. And because of this they're committed to giving, as they've been gifted.

They are a beautiful couple. Won't it be wonderful, I've thought, for them to share their wisdom with the next generation? Then, voila! The baby was a girl!

So even adults have to wrestle with the challenge of being generous. Even adults have to work to face the truth that they've been gifted, and that they should try to gift others in return.

In my work, I discuss many ethical issues with many different kinds of people, and I often find myself returning to this question of generosity. The people I work with are good people, people who recognize that they've been gifted. For them the question is not whether to give, but rather how much. So I ask them: "How much of their annual income do you think people ought to give away?" I explain that when I speak of "annual income," I don't mean some technical figure such as the "adjusted gross income" on the income tax form. I'm talking simply. "From all the money received in a year, from whatever source, what percentage do you believe a person ought to give away?"

I get many different answers. Some people whose morality is shaped by the Bible embrace the practice of tithing. One woman answered me very simply. "Everything that I have was given to me by God. So really, none of it is actually mine. And of all that God gives me, God allows me to keep and use 90 percent. I think that's pretty generous of God! All God asks is that I give back 10 percent. So I don't even think of that money as mine. I just pass it along, as God asks me to do."

Most people, however, aren't willing to propose tithing. Not only do they not give away that much money themselves, they're not prepared to say they think people should give that much away. Actually, the most common response I receive is that people ought to give away the equivalent of 3 percent of their income.

The phrase "3 percent" sounds small, I know. What a tiny portion of one's wealth! And when I ask people if such a percentage strikes them as reasonable (especially if I don't give them time to do the multiplication in order to calculate what this would mean for them!), they usually think it's quite modest. But if we translate this percentage into dollars, it doesn't sound so insignificant. A person whose total income is $33,000, for example, would be giving away a thousand dollars a year. And a family with income, from all sources, of $70,000 would be donating over $2,000. So maybe this percentage would be a rather good goal, after all.

And it would be a goal! When I ask people, candidly, if their current charity meets this standard, many have to admit that it does not. What may be even more troubling, when I ask them to tell me the percentage that is true (perhaps through an anonymous questionnaire), I find that the percentage named by those of modest means—even people who make much less than the amounts I've used as examples—is often higher than that of the wealthy.

It would be a good thing, I believe, if this conversation could be expanded. Ask yourself, first of all. What percentage do you think ought to be shared? What percentage do you now give?

Then ask your friends. If you don't want to be too intrusive, skip the second question. Just ask your friends and relatives what amount, as a percentage of all income received in a year, ought to be shared with people and causes in need. See what they say. Then let the conversation move to the questions we've looked at in these pages. What is generosity? How do we join the truth that we've done a good job with the truth that we've built on gifts we've received from others?

———⋖✦⋗———

In the end, I don't think that money questions are really about money. They're about power, as we saw at the beginning of this chapter. They're about what we want and how bad we want it.

Even more deeply, money questions are about our understanding of ourselves. Do I view myself as unconnected to other people, as completely independent? If so, my attitude regarding money will be clear: It's mine, and I'll do with it what I want. Or do I view myself as interconnected with other people in myriad mysterious ways? Do I see that everything I am has come to me from others: my talents, my expertise, my health, my opportunities? Perhaps I've used these gifts well, but they were gifts nonetheless. If this is my view, then I'll feel a responsibility to do for others what's been done for me, to give gifts as I've received gifts.

And then, when they show me the money, I'll know what to do with it!

———⋖✦⋗——— ———⋖✦⋗——— ———⋖✦⋗———

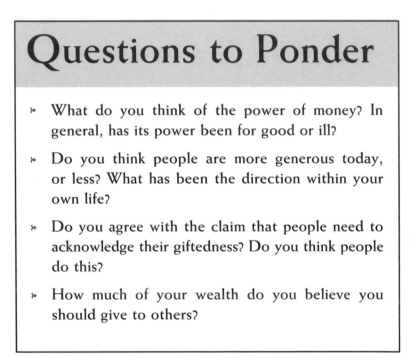

Questions to Ponder

❧ What do you think of the power of money? In general, has its power been for good or ill?

❧ Do you think people are more generous today, or less? What has been the direction within your own life?

❧ Do you agree with the claim that people need to acknowledge their giftedness? Do you think people do this?

❧ How much of your wealth do you believe you should give to others?

Parents Are Forever

The scene was funny. Clare is twenty-five, a beautiful, self-confident young woman living in her own apartment up in the city. But here she was, spending an evening at her parents' house, struggling down the stairs with one of the largest piles of dirty laundry I've ever seen. Off to the parental washing machine, it seems.

Then, going out with some friends to listen to music, there was a whispered query. "Mom, do you have any money?" Uncle Tim slipped her a few dollars; he knows the path to a young person's heart!

Her mother brought up the episode the next morning. "Thanks for the bail-out," she said. "You didn't have to do that, you know." Then she went on.

"It's really strange," she said, "the way parenting just won't end. They're adults, after all. You can't tell them what to do. But I've noticed that when they say 'home,' they don't mean wherever they live. They mean here. It's not just the dirty laundry and a few free bucks, either. It's something deeper, a lot deeper.

"And I thought it would all be over by now!"

It's not over, of course, not ever. Religious traditions describe certain events that change one forever, causing some sort of "ontological change," as they call it. That's the way it is with parenting, too. It's possible, of course, to father a baby, to bear a child, without becoming a parent, as I'm using the term. But if you really become a parent, deciding that this child is yours in every important sense of that word, then it never ends. If you agree to help in the task of parenting our world, even in some alternative mode, then it never ends. Parents are forever.

The everyday struggles of parenting are forever, too. The tough choices that try to shape and guide, to encourage and confront, and in a hundred different ways to help them grow into good and responsible adults—these never end for those who really are parents. So while parents wrestle with all the other issues we've considered in these pages, the issues of job or community, of their own sexuality and of the needs of the poor, they also wrestle with the issues of parenting itself. And they wrestle with them forever.

Years ago I saw the movie, *Witness*, set in an Amish settlement in the Midwest. I don't remember much about the plot; I was more taken with the texture of Amish life than with the story itself. There's something so enticing about an isolated group, keeping its own wholesome ways against destructive intrusions. The group protects its values, maintains its traditions, honors its past, and passes on its vision. Most pointedly, the group raises its kids to share the same values.

It doesn't work that easily, of course, for the Amish or for any of us. The outer world is there. It can be resisted, but it can't be denied; and sooner or later its presence will be felt. So parents struggle, trying to raise their kids, instilling the values that are theirs and passing on the vision that they cherish, in the face of the competing values and visions that are available in the world today.

And they do it forever. Parents are forever, and so are the tough choices that they face. Here, if anywhere, good people face tough choices, and they face them forever. Let's see what light we can bring to this uniquely important endeavor of all of our human projects.

⊰•◦•⊱

After years of research, scholars have come to understand rather fully how it happens that values are passed from parents to children, from one generation to the next. Their conclusions are not particularly surprising, and they're also not particularly encouraging to all of us who are less than perfect. For the simple truth is that approaches to life are absorbed through a process of observation and imitation. And the ones being observed and imitated are us!

First of all, observation takes place. Think of this: None of us is traveling through life for the second time. For every one of us, it's the first time we've ever been here. So we all have a sense of newness in our lives, of not knowing for sure how life is meant to be lived, of how we should handle the challenges coming at us for the first time. We have convictions, of course. But since none of us has completed the great circuit of life, we can't claim to have proved, in the outcome of our own living, that our convictions are on target.

How do we deal with this sense of "not yet"? We watch one another like hawks. We look for people who appear to be successful at life, not just at particular activities but even more at the overarching activity of being a human person. We look for people near the end of their lives, people who have remained faithful to a vision of life and who appear to have confirmed that vision in their own living. We look for people who have succeeded by whatever measure we choose to use: wealth, recognition, peacefulness, joy, love. In a special way, we look for people just a little older than ourselves, people who have just completed negotiating the specific challenges that face us now, who seem to have done a good job of being the age we are about to be. Yes, we look for these people, and we watch them like hawks.

Then we imitate those people, all of us, young and old alike.

The youngsters among us may imitate their hero quite slavishly. They may dress like their hero or try to walk like their hero. They may adopt the hero's way of speaking or style of grooming. They may decide to eat the same cereal, drive the same car, join the same church as their hero. In doing all this, the youngsters hope that they will succeed in life in just the same way as the hero has. I live in Chicago, home to the Chicago

Bulls basketball team and, most particularly, to Michael Jordan, superstar without peer. In our town we have a veritable industry of Jordania, products that allow the purchaser to imitate this hero of the courts. Buyers stand in line for the privilege of just this sort of absolute imitation.

For those of us who are a bit older, the imitation may be somewhat more subtle, but it's just as real. We may not dress exactly like our hero all the time. But look at groups of friends out for a social evening. As the camera pans the crowd at a sports event, notice the team paraphernalia that so many are wearing. Walk through the halls of corporate America and observe the matching ties and scarves! We may not eat exactly the same food, but what about the brand of beer—or designer water—that people select? We may not walk just like the hero, but we may appropriate the same daily schedule, arriving early or staying late at work, organizing different chores similarly, devoting the weekend to similar pursuits. Our reason for undertaking this nuanced imitation? It's the same as the reason for the young people's slavish imitation. It's the hope that by so doing we may succeed in life as our model quite obviously has.

Who are the people in your life who've been the object of your observation and imitation? Who are the heroes in your life? And has your imitation achieved its purpose, leading you to succeed as your model succeeded?

In our own lives, we've picked up attitudes and skills through a process of observation and imitation, and we know this will occur in the lives of our children, too. So in doing the work

103

of parenting, we try to provide models they can observe and imitate. The first model for our children is, of course, ourselves. What a scary thought!

The young people in my vicinity are not listening to my well-spoken and truly meant instructions. They're just watching me, to see how I actually do it! They're seeing my acts of charity, my efforts of perseverance, my words of compassion, my commitments of effort. But they're also seeing my moments of meanness, my walls of unconcern, my gestures of anger, my choices of selfishness. They observe it all, and to the extent that I look successful to them, a person to be imitated, they may well elect to imitate it all. So this is a problem. As good as I may in some ways be, I'm not consistent in being the kind of person I want to be, and the children can't be shielded from that fact.

But at least this problem can be dealt with. I can—I must—work harder at being the kind of person I'd want them to imitate. Paradoxically, I can forget about the children and work at being the kind of person I truly want to be. In doing that, I can present the kind of model I'd like them to see. Indeed, in the end, nothing is more important to the project of raising the kids than this: to work strenuously and consistently at the project of one's own life. It can appear selfish, this attention to one's own journey. But it's not. Growing in wisdom, expanding in balance, deepening in commitment, blossoming in gentleness and humor—all this is not only a service to the self. It's also the key to raising our kids as we should.

I invite you to look, then, at the various sectors of your life. Try to float above the scene, so to speak, and observe how things transpire. Watch your actions in the home. Do you embody the approach to life you hope they will enact? Trace the lines of your behavior on the job. Even when you're alone, do you act as you'd have them one day act? Follow your travels around the community, in the car, at the store, within the confines of church or synagogue or mosque. Is the person you see there the person you hope they will be?

While you're at it, take a good look at how you act in the very act of parenting. Last summer I attended a baseball game involving one of the youth leagues. For the most part it was a pleasant, even exciting experience. But the game was painfully marred by the behavior of one of the dads. At first it seemed he was simply cheering on his son, as all the parents were doing. But then his shouts became more strident, his demands more intense. Little by little it became clear that the father was deeply invested in this game in ways that had nothing to do with his son's pleasure in sport or development of physical ability. It was the father's desire to win that was driving his comments, his self esteem that was at stake, his dreams of glory that hung in the balance. The son's interests had been utterly and irrevocably lost.

I had several reactions. One, of course, was sadness at the pressure this was placing upon this young person. How unfair to ask a child to meet his parent's personal needs! Another was fear that this boy's inevitable observation of his father's behavior would truly lead to imitation, so that the boy would grow up thinking that this is actually how parenting is meant to be. We know that an amazingly high percentage of those who abuse children were themselves abused as children. In smaller but just as truly destructive ways, adults who use parenting for their own ends were probably used themselves to meet their parents' needs.

That's why the first challenge is so important, this challenge that is really very simple even if it's excruciatingly difficult. Tend the garden of your own life, since that life is the one most immediately available to your children for observation and imitation.

⊰◆⊱

Kids develop their attitudes and behaviors through a process of observation and imitation. But the objects of their observation are many, and that can't be avoided. Here, I think, lies the sad verdict on the efforts of the Amish and of others like them. So deeply do they cherish their values, that they try to protect their children from any other examples of living. But in the end it can't be done. Perhaps the other examples can be kept at a distance for a while, and maybe that's worth the effort. But they cannot finally be excluded. And if that's true of the Amish, it's even more true for the rest of us, who live in more cosmopolitan settings.

Consider, for example, the school setting. Universal education, that glory of the American scene, was first established in the attempt to maximize the process of passing knowledge from one generation to the next. In that sense, universal education was intended to make the older generation more influential in the lives of youth than it ever before had been, communicating more effectively than ever important insights about the meaning of life and the tasks of adulthood.

But think about that school setting. If it's true that we absorb values through observation and imitation, who is the most consistently available source for this observation? Is it the teacher? No, the students get a new teacher each year. Is it the writers of textbooks? Hardly. Textbooks come and go, with only the most superficial impact on the students. Well, then, who is it? The other students, of course! From the age of six until the age of eighteen, the only consistent thing in many children's lives is the fellow students in their grade. When observation is to be done, it's the behavior of the peers that is observed. And when imitation begins to occur, it's, not surprisingly, the ways of the peers that are most consistently imitated.

So here's the irony: that a system designed to maximize the impact of one generation upon the next has, in fact, maximized the impact of the peer group and, if anything, marginalized the impact of the adult community upon young people.

What follows from this is that the first competition you'll face in your efforts at parenting, as you try to provide models for observation and imitation, will be the other children. And as I've already pointed out, you can't eliminate that competition. You can, at best, engage it at specific, critical moments.

A colleague of mine, who's the father of three teenagers, said it plainly, if poignantly. "The teens have so many quirks. I may not like lots of the things they do, but I have to pick my battles. Does my daughter come down to dinner with purple hair?

I may have to let that pass (though God forbid she should know that in advance!). But a ring through her nose? Now, that may be a moment to draw a line in the sand!" One way or another, all of us who wish to pass along our values to the next generation must make similar judgments.

———⊰•⊱———

In addition to the power of the peer group in providing uninvited models for observation and imitation, the other unavoidable influence is the media. You don't have to be in the same room with another person to engage in the process of observation and imitation. You simply have to be somehow in contact with that person. The instruments of mass media are very effective at providing that contact. Every time I turn on the television, I'm presented with potential role models.

These role models may be real people, people who live far away but who are brought near to me through the technology of television. They may be sports figures, actors, musicians of various stripes, cultural icons from across the land and around the world. They may be the local senator, the committed doctor fighting hunger in the Sudan, the leader of a hate group, proud to spout his venom for the camera. Or they may be the rather odd, often pathetic people who inhabit the daytime talk shows.

Never before have we been made so aware of the alternative patterns of life that are available for choice in our world. Children today know, from a very early age, that the way things are done in their family is not the only way they can be done. So their choices are very clear to them, and if we try to pretend otherwise, if we try to pretend that our way is evidently the only good way, even the only imaginable way, we reveal to our children not our wisdom but our naivete. They know better.

As if this array of real-life options were not enough, young people are also presented a stunning array of fictional characters as potential objects of observation and imitation. Often enough, indeed, this is a wonderful gift.

Just recently I happened upon an evening drama involving your typical, hard-boiled police detective—who, at this moment, had an unusual problem. Long divorced, he was about to introduce his new love, with whom he was planning marriage, to his son. His love for his son was clear in the fact that he was visibly anxious about this impending meeting, not wanting to hurt the son, actually hoping to receive his blessing. They came together. But the son, it turned out, was also anxious. He had something to talk about, something that he, too, was approaching with fear and trembling. Before the detective could even begin to share the news of his wedding, the son blurted out that he had decided to join the army. Would his dad approve? Could he get his dad's blessing?

It was a beautiful moment, professionally and sensitively crafted. As these two men reached out and, in hesitant words, communicated their mutual love and respect, as they assured each other of their best wishes, a wonderful lesson was taught. I was touched. In fact, I was doubly touched, both by the genuine warmth of the story and by the power-for-good that television can provide.

It's not always so, of course. The stories that are told can also be stories of shabbiness. They can present lifestyles of meanness, of selfishness and indulgence, of cruelty and indifference. And these stories, just as surely, offer models for the viewer to consider.

—————————

Yes, the stories presented on television offer models of living, all enticing, though in many different ways.

This isn't a new thing, really. Stories have long been used to present models for imitation. Religious bodies, ethnic and national groups, families and tribes have all used stories of heroic action as a way of commending—by demonstrating—admirable behavior to the listening audience. They've also used stories of violence and deceit as cautionary tales, portraying life alternatives to be avoided and rejected by persons of good will.

What's new in the television situation, then? Two things are new. One new thing is the way the stories are distributed in our culture and the massive exposure that inevitably results. The characters of the soap operas or of the evening dramas are well known to our children. From one end of the country to the other, children can describe in detail who these people are, what they are doing, and why they are doing it.

The other thing that's new is the way the stories are brought into the privacy of many homes, all at the same time. In times gone by, stories were told in public, communal settings. As a result, the members of the audience always had two sets of information to work with, the content of the story and the reactions of other audience members. All the time they were watching the play or listening to the tale, they were also participating in a subtle but quite audible act of evaluation. Did they, as a group, approve of the character's behavior? Their cheers or boos would tell. Did they find the joke humorous, or was it in bad taste? The laughter or the groan would make that clear. Now, with many individuals watching the same show in the isolation of their living rooms, this second source of information is missing. So if I find the joke to be vulgar, there's a tendency for me to presume it's my problem, that the story is right and I am wrong. And I have no one to tell me otherwise.

Yes, television is history's most powerful storyteller. At the same time, television's isolated, alienated audience is the most powerless that's ever existed. And there's no simple way to remedy this. Turning off the stories at their source, perhaps by turning off the television, is a short-term solution at best. Parents of smaller children, for example, do have to exercise this minimal control, and postponing some issues can be a helpful thing. Still, it's only a temporary measure.

But there is something we all can do. We can talk. If you want to do battle with the stories that come from television, try the stimulated conversation. For through conversation the audience-as-group can be recreated, the power of the second set of information can be reestablished.

Several months ago, I sat with a group of friends as we watched an evening drama. It was a fairly sleazy story, filled with sexual escapades, broken promises, casual deceit, and abiding selfishness. It was also, I must admit, enormously entertaining! The show ended, and we adjourned to the kitchen for popcorn and soda. "What'd you think of that?" someone asked.

An amazing conversation ensued. Everyone had opinions, and not all agreed. But we all cared about real values, we all wanted to think about how people really should live, we all felt the questions about life that the show had implicitly raised. We talked for quite a while, and a wonderful evening became the occasion for wonderful learnings, as well.

That's the power of conversation. The addictive aspect of stories is that the listener tends to presume they are true; and if there's a dissonance between the lifestyle of the characters and my lifestyle, the tendency will be to presume that I am the one in error. Conversation can neutralize that presumption. Conversation can instead confirm the quiet suspicion that the TV story is false, that this is not really how life works, that people like this are not, in the end, truly admirable. Thus, conversation can lead viewers to look elsewhere, back in the real world, for the kinds of models they want.

So there's a lesson here for us. We have to attend to the stories presented by popular culture. We can't avoid them. Perhaps when we would most prefer to turn off the TV and to

ignore the schlock we perceive there, we must instead force ourselves to stay tuned. For at the least, we can't compete with stories we don't even know.

Then, building on what we know, we can stimulate
the conversation.

———◆———

Yes, parents are forever. And the key to successful
parenting, we've seen, is the providing of models for observation
and imitation.

Doing this involves many things. First, it involves tending
to our own affairs, struggling at the most central of everyday
struggles, the project of growing as a person. Second, it involves
the generous, and tremendously wise, practice of providing lots
of other positive models. Don't try to hog the limelight. Instead,
let your children join groups where they'll meet other inspiring
adults, let them have dinner at their friends' houses to see the gifts
those parents possess, let them cultivate relationships with admirable
teachers, caring coaches, upright and inspirational neighbors.

Third, pay careful attention to the peers with whom they
associate. Never underestimate the observation that's going on as
they play together, study together, go on outings together. Don't
try to isolate your children from peers; that will only cultivate
rebellion in them. Instead, try to increase the number of relationships they have by placing them in a growing variety of groups.

Joining sports teams and scout groups, participating in summer Bible camps and recreation programs, all these are important. And the actual activity involved is only part of the importance. Also important—maybe even more important—is the sharing, the observation and imitation that goes on while the activity is pursued.

Finally, allow stories to have their full power. Tell stories of heroes in your family and in your history. Help your children develop the wonderful habit of reading, where their imaginations can be stimulated for a process of observation and imitation in the heart. Watch pictorial stories with them, going to the movies, sitting in front of the TV, sharing rented videos. Even when the stories are dubious, don't necessarily turn them off. Instead, experience them and then talk about them. Let your children also observe you engaging challenging stories, so that they can imitate your open but critical response.

Yes, there are many things that can nurture this process of observation and imitation. All of them can help you succeed in the forever challenge of parenting.

And if you do succeed in this powerful human project, then you will have been victorious in what is perhaps the most important of all the tough choices that good people face.

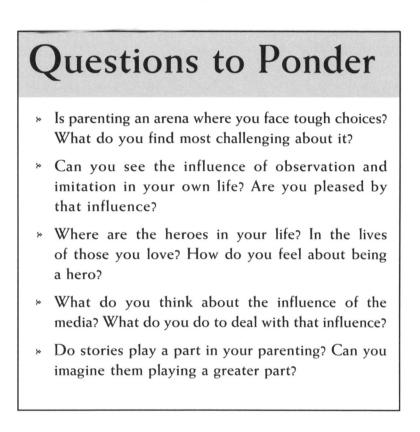

Questions to Ponder

- Is parenting an arena where you face tough choices? What do you find most challenging about it?

- Can you see the influence of observation and imitation in your own life? Are you pleased by that influence?

- Where are the heroes in your life? In the lives of those you love? How do you feel about being a hero?

- What do you think about the influence of the media? What do you do to deal with that influence?

- Do stories play a part in your parenting? Can you imagine them playing a greater part?

8

Struggling Together

The title of this book declares that it's for good people. The claim is quite intentional, for I believe that just this sort of people will be attracted to it. People who are not good, who are not trying to live with care and concern, don't waste their time on the challenges of tough choices. Only good people do that. This book is for them—for you—in order to help you in dealing with the challenge of facing your decisions.

In the chapters of this book we've looked at various arenas of our lives, places where these tough choices take place. In the ideas and the stories that have been presented, we've tried to find light for our journey, strength for our effort, insight and encouragement for the work we can't escape. And in the first chapter we saw that these tough choices are not once-in-a-while things. Rather, they are everyday struggles, unavoidable threads in the fabric that makes up our lives.

Now I offer one last set of considerations. On the one hand, they add an important understanding of why we find these tough choices of ours so remarkably difficult. On the other hand, they offer what I believe to be a most useful collection of final suggestions, ideas about how we can respond more and more successfully to these everyday struggles.

For I do believe that being the kind of person we want to be is harder in today's world than it's ever been before. Why's that? The reason is that for many members of today's human community, life is frightfully anonymous. More than has ever before been the case in human history, we're often away from those who know and love us. Especially for those who live in cities, but to some extent for all of us, part of the landscape of our everyday struggles is this anonymous context in which they take place. And that certainly doesn't make things easier.

I'd like to believe that I would be the same sort of person whether I'm around those I know and love or not. But I know that isn't the case. For example, I work at home. If I get sleepy while I'm working, what do I do? I stop and take a nap! Would I do that if I was working in an office setting, surrounded by respected colleagues? I would not. In fact, I know I would not, since I once worked in such a setting, and I didn't just close the door and nap. Now, maybe I should have. In some cases the nap might actually have increased my productivity. But I didn't. Rather, in the presence of these valued others, I "toughed it out" and persevered in my work. By myself, on the contrary, I often give in and do quickly whatever I feel like.

I think the same could be said of most of us. In a hundred ways the solitary self behaves differently than the related self, often less honorably and sometimes less honestly, but almost always quite differently. So, if much of one's life in today's world is solitary, then this not-so-virtuous way of living can easily become the norm rather than the exception in our personal patterns of behavior. And if this happens, then responding to our everyday struggles will surely become more difficult than it used to be.

Think of a helium-filled balloon. Since helium is lighter than air, the balloon stretches upward, pulling against the string to which it's attached. I imagine that if the balloon could talk, it would declare: "Set me free! This string is holding me back, frustrating my attempts to be who I truly am. This connection prevents my personal flourishing." But imagine that the balloon's wish is fulfilled, and the string is released. Up, up the balloon goes. As it rises, it moves to altitudes where the air is thinner, so that the balloon expands as the helium faces less and less resistance from the outside atmosphere. In the end, of course, the balloon explodes. It self-destructs and falls to the earth useless.

As we watch this sad comeuppance, we learn an important lesson. The string that appeared to resist what was best for the balloon was actually its best friend, and this connection between the balloon and its surroundings, far from frustrating it, was the very thing that allowed it to flourish. The balloon that was most fully and happily a balloon was not the utterly liberated, unrelated balloon, but rather the connected balloon. Indeed, an unconnected balloon is, in the end, no balloon at all.

It's the same with us humans. So often we experience our relationships as inhibiting. We imagine that we could flourish much more fully if we were freed from these connections. But the opposite is the case. Apart from our relationships, we hardly exist at all; and apart from our relationships, we certainly never become our best selves.

Indeed, if the truth be told, I'm my best self not out of isolated pride or autonomous self-esteem, but rather out of concern for those I love. I would not disappoint them. It would make me very sad to betray their expectations of me. So I'm challenged by their presence, even more by their love, to reach for the best, to do always the good, and so to be the sort of person I believe they'd want me to be.

How difficult this is, though, in a culture that's as anonymous as ours. At least for those of us who live in cities or travel with any regularity, we spend much of our lives in settings where we're not known. So we're faced with challenges in situations where no one important to us will ever know how they're answered. There's the challenge to do our job conscientiously, but no one will ever know. There's the challenge to be faithful to marital commitments, but no one will ever know. There's the challenge to treat those around us with fairness and respect and compassion, but no one will ever know. How hard it is to be our best selves at such moments.

What areas of your life are most susceptible to the temptations of anonymity? It could be the office setting, where no one knows whether the yellow scratch pad slips into your briefcase or whether the long-distance phone call is business related or whether the reading going on is in service to the job. It could be the neighborhood, where no one knows whether you sort your garbage for recycling or respond to requests to limit the use of electricity and to forgo watering the lawn or pay for the newspaper you snatch from the doorstep as you leave for work. It could be in public spaces, where prohibitions of littering or requests for quiet or the commands of traffic signals can so easily be ignored.

In all these areas we need to face this new problem, this situation of being anonymous, and we need to try to remedy it. For the simple truth is this: to address successfully the everyday struggles that confront us, we need to be struggling together.

———————

It's a common phrase, and a true one: to live our best, we all need moral support. We need to find in others the strength to be our best selves and to act in the most caring manner. We need to know we are struggling together. But that's not all we need.

This book started by facing the fact that, like my cherished friends, Grace and Charlie Oatley, we often feel caught by the tough choices that face us. It's often the case that we really do want to do what's right, what would truly be helpful to those around us. If we needed moral support, we've somehow already received it. Now the challenge isn't that of choosing to do the good, it's that of knowing what is the good that I should choose.

So the book set out to address that problem. In fact, as I've several times pointed out, this book is really for people who've already decided to be good. After all, only good people are willing to take the time to read about and think about every-day struggles. But that means that even good people need something to handle their tough choices. What is it they need? Why, they need insight into what the good looks like, into the best way to come to understand the good, into strategies for dealing with the competition of goods in our finite world. So this book has tried to provide that sort of assistance, too, not only support for our good will but also resources to our good thinking.

As this book comes to a close, I want to make it very clear that you and I will also continue to need this second sort of assistance in the future. The string that attaches the balloon to the fencepost and thereby allows it to survive is not just that network of expectations that calls us to be our best selves. It's also that circle of wisdom that helps us find the best thing to do. And just as the lack of others' expectations means we may well not behave as we really should, just as surely does the lack of others' wisdom mean we may well not achieve the truly helpful good we genuinely desire.

Yes, we all need communities of wisdom. So true is this, that most of the great religious traditions have argued that personal decisions made in isolation are almost certainly not the wisest decisions we could make. Christians hear the statement of Jesus: "Where two or three are gathered in my name, I am there among them," and they understand it as a call to confide in one another and to find in one another both strength and wisdom for human living (Matthew 18:20). Roman Catholics may implement this truth through an elaborate mechanism of Church teaching. Mainline Protestants may emphasize discussions within the local congregation. Evangelicals may depend on a prayerful consideration of individual Bible verses. Quakers may convene quiet fellowships of discernment. But they're all building on the same conviction and seeking the same wise goal.

We find similar insights in other religions. In yeshivas, ordinary Jews encounter the riches of Talmudic wisdom and the insights of their own common study. In the monasteries of the Buddhist and Hindu traditions this reality of a community of shared discernment is daily enacted. And when Muslims fall to the earth together in long lines, facing Mecca in a common posture of prayerful attention, and when they rise to go their various ways, all the while sharing the discipline of their Ramadan fast, the same thing is happening. It's partly communal support, of course. But it's also a structure of communal insight, to help illumine the tough choices that will inevitably complicate for good people the living of every day.

I wonder if you can see the same pattern in the ordinary events of your life. I look out the front window of my office and I see people walking their dogs. They stop and chat. They talk about their pets, then about keeping the sidewalks clean, then about the broader challenges of city living. Soon enough, they're sharing their wisdoms about life in today's world. I wouldn't be surprised if things like this happen to you. Communities of discernment happen at the oddest moments, in the most surprising places. In grocery check-out lines, around weekend breakfast tables, while riding in the car or raking the leaves, suddenly communities of discernment are quietly, almost unconsciously convened. But whenever and wherever they take place, the rich food of varied wisdom is served, and everyone walks away nourished.

And in that moment it once again becomes clear that we do our best with our everyday struggles when we find a way to struggle together.

Here, I think, lies a crucially important lesson for us, for all of us who seek to live well in this complicated world. What is that lesson? Make sure that you struggle together.

Don't give in to the forces of anonymity. The pull toward isolation is attractive, to be sure. But it's a centrifugal force. It pulls us away from the center of our reality. It draws us farther and farther from the neighbors who give us strength and light, and it runs the risk of throwing us forth into a free fall of stupidity and weakness, of violence and self-destruction. Instead, embrace the forces of relationship.

I know that not all relationships are healthy. Some, to be sure, cause their own sorts of violence and self-destruction. There are some relationships that are nothing but death-dealing, masked in a costume of care. For them, there's no healthy response except escape. But even then, real escape is not a flight into isolation. Rather, it's an emigration into other, better and more life-giving relationships.

I also know that relationships are no substitute for developing our own personhoods. I've known people who run frantically from one dependent relationship to another, thinking that they can't be complete unless they're tied to someone else. The truth is that relationships only succeed when they join persons who are already whole.

I know, too, that men and women typically sort out the tensions of individuality and relationship in different ways. The stereotype—which is often true—is that women face more of a challenge in developing autonomy, men in accepting dependence. Still, for all of us, the interdependence that provides moral support and moral insight is something we can't do without.

So for all of us the truth remains, that to respond successfully to our everyday struggles, we need to embrace the positive power of relationship. We need to struggle together.

Precisely because we are good people—who do not always find it easy to be good. Precisely because we face tough choices—with no obvious and evident solutions. Precisely because in this most human of worlds, we will always face everyday struggles. Precisely because of all this, we must try always to struggle together.

That's the suggestion. It's the need that prompted you to pick up this book. It's the learning you can take with you at the end.

The Hebrew scriptures tell the wonderful story of Elisha, the prophet, who had reached a point where the everyday struggles of his life were just too much for him. He prayed that he might die, and so be set free at last. Under a broom tree he fell asleep, so exhausted was he from his efforts.

Suddenly, Elisha was awakened by an angel, who pointed out magical food set out at his side for a meal. "Get up and eat," the angel instructed. So Elisha ate this unexplained food, and fell asleep again. After a while, he was once more awakened; and again he found the food laid out for his meal. This time the angel was more pointed: "Get up and eat, otherwise the journey will be too much for you." Elisha did as he was instructed, and he ate the food provided.

The scriptures end this story with one of the most wonderful single lines that I know: "Then he went in the strength of that food forty days and forty nights, to Horeb, the mountain of God." (1 Kings 19:4–8)

At the table of human community we are nourished with the food of mutual support and accumulated wisdom. With the strength of that food, we can cross the desert of human complexity. We can face our everyday struggles, the tough choices that plague even the good people in our midst, the good people that we are. And we can learn to face them well. Buoyed by the strength of that food, we can reach the promised land of life. We can find a way to love one another both truly and wisely, to care for ourselves and to respect one another, to enjoy the project of our own lives and to nurture the lives of our children. With the strength of that food, we can find our way home, as surely as did Elisha, the prophet.

It's been a good thing, to walk together a while in these pages.

Godspeed!

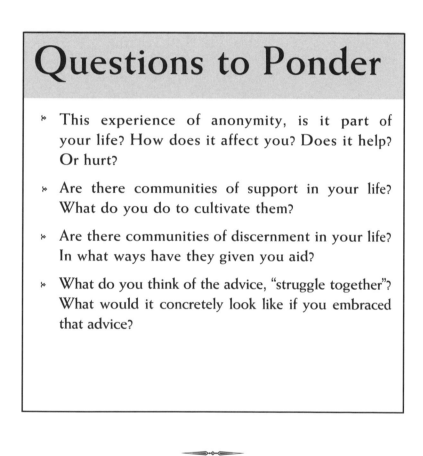

Questions to Ponder

* This experience of anonymity, is it part of your life? How does it affect you? Does it help? Or hurt?

* Are there communities of support in your life? What do you do to cultivate them?

* Are there communities of discernment in your life? In what ways have they given you aid?

* What do you think of the advice, "struggle together"? What would it concretely look like if you embraced that advice?

TIMOTHY E. O'CONNELL, PH.D., is a professor of pastoral studies at Loyola University in Chicago. A widely known author and speaker, Dr. O'Connell is the author of *Tend Your Own Garden: How to Raise Great Kids*, also published by Thomas More. *Good People, Tough Choices* is the second in this series of books specifically geared to the everyday needs of ordinary families. Future books in this series will address the challenges of maintaining a personal spirituality amid life's pressures.

Timothy O'Connell welcomes the reflections of his readers. You may contact him by mail at:

Institute of Pastoral Services
Loyola University Chicago
6525 N. Sheridan Road
Chicago, IL 60626

You may also contact him by e-mail at:

toconne@luc.edu